CALIFORNIA'S HIGH WINDSHIELD ADVENTURING

A GUIDE TO ATTRACTIONS FOUND ALONG, AND ACCESSIBLE OFF OF THE 385 MILES OF HIGHWAY 395 FROM HIGHWAY I-15 IN THE SOUTH TO THE NEVADA BORDER. A TRIP FROM THE HIGH DESERT IN THE SOUTH AND THROUGH THE HIGH SIERRAS.

By Russell and Kathlynn Spencer

3600 South Harbor Blvd. #338
Oxnard, CA. 93035
Web site: www.windshieldadventures.com

ISBN# 0-9664055-9-5

Printed by:

Wilson Printing
Ventura, CA - 805-654-9494
www.wilprint.com

First Edition
COPYRIGHT 2002 by Russell & Kathlynn Spencer

All rights reserved except as noted below. No part of this book may be reproduced in any form or by any electronic or mechanical means including information storage and retrieval systems without permission in written form from the publisher, except by a reviewer who may quote brief passages in a review.

ISBN# 0-9664055-9-0

Library of Congress Number Pending

Other books by the authors:
*Mojave Desert Windshield Adventures
(ISBN# 0-9664055-8-7}
Windshield Adventuring along California's Central Coast
(ISBN# 0-9964055-6-0)
Windshield Adventuring in Southern & Central Nevada
(ISBN# 0-9664055-4-4)
Windshield Adventuring through the Mojave Desert
(ISBN# 0-9664055-1-X)

Updated Spring, 2006

Use of graphic and other materials contained in this book, which were obtained from sources other than the authors, is excluded from the copyright of this material by the authors

*Revised portions of *Mojave Desert Windshield Adventures* are contained herein as a portion of this work

TABLE OF CONTENTS

	PAGE
INTRODUCTION	a
GUIDE TO USING THIS BOOK	b
HIGHWAY 395, A BRIEF HISTORY	d
THE EASTERN SIERRA BYWAY	e
RV CAMPING SITES	95
CAMPING GUIDELINES	99
INFORMATION POINTS: MUSEUMS, VISITORS CENTERS, WEB SITES, ETC.	102
INDEX	106

SECTION ONE HIGHWAY 395 FROM I-15 AT HESPERIA TO INDEPENDENCE
207 MILES

	PAGE
OUTLINE OF *LOOP TRIPS A, B & C*	1
MAP OF SECTION ONE	2
HESPERIA, DOBY CORNERS, ADELANTO, EL MIRAGE DRY LAKE	3
SHADOW MOUNTAIN ROAD, KRAMER JUNCTION	4
THE "RAND" RED MOUNTAIN, RANDSBURG, JOHANNESBURG	5
DESCRIPTION *LOOP SIDE TRIPS "A" & "B"* CHINA LAKE ROAD	7
RIDGECREST, MATURANGO MUSEUM, CHINA LAKE NAVAL AIR STATION, JUNCTION OF STATE ROUTE 14, TERMINATION OF *LOOP TRIP "A"*	8
OWENS VALLEY	9
PEARSONVILLE, KENNEDY MEADOWS, LITTLE LAKE, FOSSIL FALLS	10
COSO JUNCTION, OLANCHA, JNCT. HWY 190, LOOP SIDE TRIP "C"	11
OWENS LAKE, COTTONWOOD CHARCOAL KILNS	12
JNCT. HWY 136, INTERAGENCY VISITORS CENTER, LONE PINE, TERMINATION OF *LOOP TRIP "B"*	13
ALABAMA HILLS	14
WHITNEY PORTALS	15
MANZANAR NATIONAL HISTORIC SITE MAP	16
MANZANAR NATIONAL HISTORIC SITE	17
INDEPENDENCE, EASTERN CALIFORNIA MUSEUM, KEARSARGE AND MAZURKA CANYON	18

LOOP SIDE TRIP "A" PAGES 20 TO 25
RANDSBURG WEST TO I-14 TO RED ROCK CANYON NORTH TO 395

JUNCTION HWY 14, JAWBONE STATION BLM INFORMATION CENTER	20
RED ROCK CANYON STATE PARK	21
RED ROCK INYO-KERN RD. EL PASO MOUNTAINS BURROW SCHMIDTS TUNNEL	22
SCHMIDT'S TUNNEL ACCESS MAP	23
SCHMIDT'S TUNNEL ACCESS, ROBBER'S ROOST	24
HIGHWAY 178 WEST, LAKE ISABELLA ACCESS, HIGHWAY 178 EAST	25

LOOP SIDE TRIP "B" PAGES 26 TO 35
RANDSBURG EAST TO TRONA PANNACLES, PANAMINT VALLEY, BALLARAT GHOST TOWN, DEATH VALLEY ACCESS, CERRO GORDO ACCESS, JOINS HWY 395 AT LONE PINE

JUNCTION HIGHWAY 178	26
TRONA PINNACLES NATIONAL MONUMENT	27
TRONA, TRONA MUSEUM	28
PANAMINT VALLEY, BALLART GHOST TOWN	29
WILDROSE CANYON ROAD, JUNCTION HIGHWAY 190	30
PANAMINT SPRINGS RESORT	31
DARWIN FALLS, ROAD TO DARWIN, JUNCTION HWYS 190 & 136	32
CERRO GORDO GHOST TOWN	33
KEELER, SWANSEA, JUNCTION HWY 395 AT LONE PINE	35

LOOP SIDE TRIP "C" PAGE 36
JUNCTION HWYS 395 & 190 AT OLANCHA
ACCESS TO LOOP TRIP "B" ACCESS TO CERRO GORDO FROM PAGE 33

DIRTY SOCKS SPRINGS, ACCESS TO HWY 190	36

SIDE TRIP TO ONION VALLEY FROM INDEPENDENCE PAGE 37 TO 38

ONION VALLEY	37

SECTION TWO INDEPENDENCE TO BISHOP (MILE 267)
60 MILES

MAP OF SECTION TWO	40
MOUNT WHITNEY FISH HATCHERY. FORT INDEPENDENCE	
COMMANDER'S HOUSE, DIVISION CREEK REST STOP	41
BIG PINE	42

SIDE TRIP HIGHWAY 168 EAST PAGES 43 TO 46
ANCIENT BRISTLECONE FOREST, ACSESS TO NEVADA HIGHWAY 95

ZURICH STATION	43
ACCESS TO DEATH VALLEY, ANCIENT BRISTLECONE FOREST	44
ACCESS TO NEVADA HIGHWAY 95	46
(END OF SIDE TRIP)	
OWENS VALLEY RADIO OBSEVATORY	46
KEOUGH'S HOT SPRINGS	47
BISHOP	48

SIDE TRIP, BISHOP CREEK CANYON AND LAKE SABRINA
PAGES 49 TO 52

CALIFORNIA HISTORIC MARKERS # 208 & 811	50

BISHOP CREEK RECREATIONAL AREA & SOUTH LAKE	50
CARDINAL, CARDINAL RESORT & LAKE SABRINA	52
LAWS MUSEUM AND HISTORICAL SITE	53

SECTION THREE
MONO COUNTY (SHERWIN GRADE TO LAKE LOPAZ)
120 MILES

SHERWIN GRADE SCENIC PULL-OUT AND SUMMIT, LAKE CRAWLEY, TOM'S PLACE AND LITTLE LAKES VALLEY	56
ROCK CREEK ROAD, ROCK CREEK LAKE & RESOTS	57
CRAWLEY LAKE ACCESS & VISTA POINT, MC GEE CREEK, BENTON CROSSING ROAD,	58
CONVICT LAKE	59
SHERWIN CREEK ROAD, HOT CREEK GEOTHERMAL SITE, HATCHERY	60
MAMMOTH LAKES (HIGHWAY 203 SOUTH END)	61
DEVILS POSTPILE	63
NORTH END MAMMOTH LAKES DR., CRESTVIEW REST AREA, OWENS RIVER ROAD	64
DEADMAN'S SUMMIT, JUNCTION GLASS FLOW & LOGGING CAMP ROADS, SOUTH END OF JUNE LAKE LOOP (HIGHWAY 158)	65
JUNCTION HWY. 120 EAST, ACCESS SOUTHERN PORTION OF MONO LAKE PANUM CRATER & SOUTH TUFA, NAVY BEACH	66
JUNCTION HWY. 158 WEST, NORTH END OF JUNE LAKE LOOP, HWY 120 WEST, TIOGA PASS TO YOSEMITE NATIONAL PARK, LEE VINING	68
MONO LAKE	69
MONO LAKE COUNTY PARK, JUNCTION 167 EAST/LUNDY LAKE AREA	72
MONO LAKE OVERLOOK, CONWAY SUMMIT	74

SIDE TRIP: VIRGINIA LAKES & DUNDERBERG AREAS
PAGES 74 TO 76

VIRGINIA CREEK, DOGTOWN	76

SIDE TRIP HIGHWAY 270 EAST, TO BODIE STATE HISTORICAL PARK
PAGES 78 TO 81

JUNCTION DUDERBERG/GREEN CREEK RD., BRIDGEPORT	82
TWIN LAKES ROAD SIDE TRIP	83
DEVIL'S GATE SUMMIT, JUNCTION HWY 108, WALKER CANYON	86
ANTELOPE VALLEY	87
WALKER, MEADOWCLIFF RESORT, COLEVILLE	88
TOPAZ, MONITOR PASS	89
LAKE TOPAZ	90

LOOP TRIP "D" PAGES 90 TO 93
HWY 120 FROM LEE VINING TO BENTON HOT SPRINGS AND BENTON
HIGHWAY 6 TO BISHOP

BENTON HOT SPRINGS	92
BENTON	93
CHALFONT	93

ACKNOWLEDGEMENTS

This book is the culmination of efforts by a number of people in addition to the authors who have simply compiled the information contained here in and added some pictures.

As always, we wish to give a special thanks to the various owners and staff of the entities which we not only barraged with questions during our visits but whom responded to our "fact check" letters which we use to verify our information prior to publishing it.

A special thanks goes to the numerous rangers and staff at the various California State Parks and National Forests which we visited during the research period of this book.

We also wish to thank The California State Parks, The National Forestry Service, The Mono Lake Committee and The Mammoth Lakes Chamber of Commerce for the use of their maps in this publication, and a special thanks to Judy Shockley for the use of her photo of earlier Mono Lake. The use of the graphic materials from the above is excluded from any and all copyrights of the material in this book by the authors.

All other material in this book is the property of the authors.

No promotional consideration was requested nor received during the creation of this work.

COVER PHOTOS: Red Rock Canyon, Rock Creek and Bodie's Church are examples of some of the attractions to be found when windshield adventuring along Highway 395!

ENJOY AND LEAVE NO TRACE!

INTRODUCTION

My first recollection of traveling up Highway 395 was at the age of 8 when my dad and I went on a fishing trip to Virginia Lakes.

Since that time I have made numerous trips up and down Highway 395 while traveling to many of the destinations accessible from it. There have been trips to Yosemite National Park, via Tioga Pass, Lake Tahoe, Reno (still enjoy the air races held at Stead) fishing sojourns along the Walker River and other bodies of water, where the trout have on occasion seen fit to enjoy the bait on my hook.

Having completed our third and fourth windshield adventuring books, "Windshield Adventuring along California's Central Coast," (ISBN# 0-9664055-6-0) and "Mojave Desert Windshield Adventures," (ISBN# 0-9664055-8-7 in 2001, it seemed only natural to share Highway 395 and its myriad of attractions.

The diversification of both the attractions and the history which surround this paved ribbon as it leaves the desert with its history of mining and becomes the access road to the back of the High Sierra Mountains, including Mount Whitney which at an altitude of 14,494 feet makes it the highest point in the continental United States, to the Walker River area, which is still recovering from the massive flood of 1968, and the more recent fires, made this unique area worth further study.

From Mono Lake with its futuristic tufas, to the ghost town of Bodie which sits in an arrested state of decay, to the spectacle of the majestic Sierras, to the antique shops and historic communities of the "Rand" to the stark statues which are the Trona Pinnacles, to the numerous lakes, streams and hot springs we will travel in this book.

Some of the attractions featured in the first section of this book were also a part of two of our previous publications; *Windshield Adventuring the Mojave Desert* and *Mojave Desert Windshield Adventures*. We have updated the information on these attractions in this book. We felt that each of our books should "stand alone" insofar as describing the features of the areas covered in the individual books.

While we are presenting the most current information possible, things do change. We sent fact verification requests to many of the entities described in the book, in addition to the fact-finding research we use in compiling the information for all of our books.

We have found that our web site, www.windshieldadventures.com, has become an excellent means of updating our readers of changes to items described in our previous travel books.

We appreciate those of you who inform us of changes, which upon verification, we can post on our web site.

A GUIDE TO USING THIS BOOK

MILEAGE: Every effort has been made to present accurate mileage between points in this book. It is important to note that there can be quite a variance between different odometers in different automobiles.

At various points we have restarted the odometer settings to zero. This has been done for several reasons. The most important reason to reset is that if an area is visited which involves driving within the attraction. We also have made recommendations for resets at points in route where loop trips begin or terminate.

LOOP TRIPS: This book contains various loop trips or "scenic routes." These loop trips will leave Highway 395 and then return to it in another area.

While all of the loop trips are shown traveling from south to north, you may wish to visit them while traveling in the other direction.

The loop trips are shown in detail at the end of the pertinent sections.

SIDE TRIPS: Side trips leave and return to Highway 395 at the same point. These side trips are shown within the trip text, or within the loop trips. The trips appearing at the end of a chapter will be noted in the text at the point where they are located along our highway.

***ROADWAY INFORMATION:* All information pertinent to the road is in capitals. Included in road information is the number of lanes, hills and areas where heavy or slow traffic is traditionally encountered. RV ALERTS, roadways that might not be suitable for larger or underpowered vehicles are also noted in capital letters.**

CALIFORNIA ROAD INFORMATION: 1 (800) 427-ROAD

NATIONAL WEATHER SERVICE LOCAL FORCAST: (760) 873-3213

SERVICES: Every effort has been made to present the reader with up-to-date facts relevant to services available. A part of the preparation of the book has been to fact-check the information contained herein. However, business, open, close and change hours and locations.

We have, for the past five years, updated our readers with changes through our website: www.windshieldadventures.com   It is our intention to continue this policy, however we must, to a certain degree, rely on our readers to assist us in updating our information.

ALTITUDE: The altitudes shown are derived from sources deemed reliable and are shown to give the reader information which may be used for comparison or other use.

Altitude sickness can be a health factor in many travelers.

RV CAMPING SITES: This book contains RV camping sites that are located along the routes of our travels. The information regarding these sites is from sources believed reliable and the producers of this book are to be held blameless for any misinformation. No promotional consideration was requested, nor obtained, during the production of this book.

CAMPING GUIDELINES: The guidelines found here are from our personal experience. The individual campers wants need may vary from the authors.

WILDLIFE VIEWING AREAS. At several locations along Highway 395 are areas which are designated as wildlife viewing areas. At these locations there are pull-off places to park. These areas are so designated because there are quite often wildlife, deer or elk, visible from these locations.

VISITING BEAR HABITAT: Much of the attractions described in the northern portion of this book are within bear habitat. At this writing the California Department of Fish and Game estimates that there are between 16,000 and 24,000 black bears living in the state of California. The California Department of Fish and Game brochure "Living with California Black Bears," available at Department of Fish and Game offices, states that people who enter bear habitat have a responsibility to the wildlife whose habitat they are sharing. More and more campgrounds and communities are adapting a "zero-tolerance" toward people who feed bears and other wildlife. People are being cited for failing to properly store food and garbage.

The Department of Fish and Game brochure also tells to avoid bears and not to run from them, but rather if a bear approaches you they recommend that you make yourself appear to be as much of a danger to the bear as possible. They tell us to stand tall wave our arms and yell or make as much noise as possible. Should a bear attack they recommend that you fight back with anything available. BE AWARE OF YOUR SURROUNDINGS!

HIGHWAY 395, A BRIEF HISTORY

Just a little over a century ago our highway was but a series of wagon roads, game trails and paths originally created by early Native Americans. As the population is various areas surrounding Highway 395 grew these paths became linked and eventually formed the highway, as we know it today.

Prior to the advent of our present freeway system Highway 395 extended from Canada to San Diego. As Interstate Highways replaced the more local roadways, many of the old state and local highways disappeared. Highway 395 no longer exists south of its current junction with Highway I-15 at Hesperia. Another example of this replacement the old Route 66, "The mother road," in many spots lies beneath the newer multi-lane highways.

From it's current southern starting point at the junction of I-15` between Cajon Summit and the community of Hesperia, the historic roadway follows the same route northward that it has since various groups of migrating Native Americans then wagon trains created it.

It doesn't seem that long ago that as a young serviceman your author pulled out of the gate of March Air Force turned west and then headed either north or south on Highway 395, now a freeway, Interstate 215.

While our highway still extends all of the way to the Canadian border, we are going to travel on it only so far as the Topaz Lake area at the California/Nevada Border.

We will travel through the high-desert area were temperatures reach 100+ degrees and into the generally snow packed High Sierra Mountains.

Our route will take us along the back of the spectacular Sierra Nevada Mountains to camping, fishing, skiing and hiking areas.

We will visit historic ghost towns, pristine lakes, natural hot springs in addition to one of the more recent active geographic areas on the continent.

At this writing there is a widening of Highway 395 in process in several areas south of Bishop

THE EASTERN SIERRA SCENIC BYWAY

1

A group called "CURES" has designated some of the more interesting areas along the northernmost 240 miles of Highway 395, from the Coso Junction Caltrans rest area in the south to Topaz Lake in the north. These locations are by marked Eastern Sierra Scenic Byway signs and contain interpretive displays.

"CURES," The Coalition for Unified Recreation in the Eastern Sierra, is an informal partnership of recreation providers, chambers of commerce, local businesses, the environmental community and local, state and federal governments who work together to educate the public in the history, nature features and attractions and preservation in the eastern Sierra area. Recreational opportunities are also presented at these sites.

Listed below are the Eastern Sierra Scenic Byway locations as of this writing. The list below includes the approximate location of the interpretive displays and a summation of the topics contained on the displays, as shown on the web site for The Eastern Sierra Byway. It must be assumed that additional locations might be designated in the future.

The byway locations shown here are listed from south to north along Highway 395. The page numbers in this book for each of the byways is noted below. The attractions shown in this book that are designated *Eastern Sierra Scenic Byway* locations by CURES, are designated in *italics*.

COSO JUNCTION REST AREA: Native Americans and Cultures Clash. The lives of Owens Valley Paiute and their clashes with the white settler. PAGE 11

DIAZ LAKE Recreation Area (South of Lone Pine) Formed by earthquake: wetlands and birds; and movies filmed near Lone Pine. PAGE 13

LONE PINE: INTER-AGENCY VISITOR CENTER: Death Valley National Park travel tips; the Great Basin and Mojave Deserts; mountain building; and Mount Whitney. PAGE 13

MANZANAR NATIONAL HISTORIC SITE: World War II Internment Camp; Ten thousand Japanese were detained here during World War II. PAGE 17

INDEPENDENCE DEHY PARK/EASTERN SIERRA MUSEUM; Historic Walking Tour: Land of little rain and rain shadow of the Sierra Nevada; life along Independence Creek; Historic Walking Tour of town includes home of Mary Austin and Courthouse; and local recreational opportunities. PAGE 18

OWENS VALLEY OVERLOOK: Winnedumah and Panoramas; The legend of Winnedumah; Panoramas of the Sierra and the Inyo; mountain peaks; and mountain-building geology.

DIVISION CREEK REST AREA: Water and Valley Wildlife; Tule elk; desert reptiles; nature's clean-up crew; The Owens Valley forced relocation march of 1863; and Owens Valley water.

BIG PINE FLAGPOLE: Bristlecone Pines and Death Valley; The earth's oldest living trees; travel tips for Death Valley National Park; Palisades Glacier; and recreational opportunities in the Big Pine area. PAGE 42

BISHOP CITY PARK: Recreational Opportunities; Outdoor sports including fishing, camping, hiking, backpacking and pack trips; sightseeing and day trips from the Bishop area.

ROUND VALLEY: The Big Mammals: Bighorn sheep, mountain lion, and migrating deer.

SHERWIN GRADE: Glaciers and Wilderness; Moraines and Glaciers; the values of wilderness; and deer migration. PAGE 57

CROWLEY LAKE: Caldera and Fishing; The Long Valley Caldera; the formation of Crowley Lake; and terrific fishing opportunities. PAGE 58

JUNCTION 203/395 AT MAMMOTH: Year-round Recreation; Devils Postpile National Monument; Skiing at Mammoth Mountain; Nordic skiing, outdoor year-round adventures; and full service resort. .PAGE 61

CRESTVIEW: High-Elevation Recreation; visitor information for Lee Vining, June Lake Loop and Mammoth Lakes.

SOUTH JUNE LAKE LOOP JUNCTION: Scenic June Lake Loop; Driving the June Lake Loop; fall colors: and winter skiing at June Mountain Ski Resort. PAGE 65

MONO CRATERS OF SANDHOUSE GRADE: Glaciers and Volcanoes; Volcanic and glacial activity; the Long Valley eruption; life of the Paiute people in Basin; and Mono Lake's water story. PAGE 66

MONO OVERLOOK ON CONWAY SUMMIT: Mono Lake, Birds, and Great Basin; Lee Vining attractions and local recreational opportunities; Mono Lake, and oasis in the desert for birds; panorama of the Sierra; and native grasses. PAGE 74

VIRGINIA CREEK, BETWEEN CONWAY SUMMIT AND BRIDGEPORT; Life in an aspen forest, fall colors; the history of wilderness. PAGE 76

JUST SOUTH OF THE ROAD TO BODIE, BETWEEN CONWAY SUMMIT AND BRIDGEPORT: Dogtown: Mining History; Boom or Bust; the largest gold nugget on the Eastern Slope was found here. PAGE 76

BRIDGEPORT PARK: Bridgeport and Historic Walking Tour; History of Bridgeport Valley and Big Meadows. This historic walk includes the Mono County Courthouse, the Historical Society Museum, the Ghost House and 22 other sites. PAGE 82

SHINGLEMILL DAY USE AREA ON WALKER RIVER: Walker River; Lahontan Cutthroat Trout; The native Lahontan Cutthroat trout; the journey of a desert river; the Walker River in the water cycle; and the early travel route across the Sierra Nevada. PAGE 86

HIGHWAY 89/TOPAZ LAKE: Geology, Fire and Wildlife; The formation of the Great Basin; the importance of fire in the ecosystem; bird inhabitants of Topaz Lake; and migration patterns of the mule deer. PAGE 90

h

Windshield Adventuring California's Highway 395

SECTION ONE
HIGHWAY 395, I-15, AT HESPERIA, TO INDEPENDENCE
207 MILES
With loop side trips:

LOOP SIDE TRIP "A"
This side trip is described in detail on Page 20.
Randsburg/Redrock Canyon Road from Randsburg, access to *Highway 14*, 21 miles, at a location 4 miles south of *Red Rock Canyon State Park*.
ATTRACTIONS:
**Jawbone Canyon, Red Rock Canyon State Park, *Burro Schmidt's famous tunnel, *Robbers Roost, *Highway 178* access to *Lake Isabella,*
(*Indicates SIDE TRIPS from LOOP TRIP).
SERVICES ON ROUTE TRIP
Camping

LOOP SIDE TRIP "B"
This side trip is described in detail on Page 26.
Trona Road just south of Red Mountain gives access northeastward to Highway 178, east of Ridgecrest, Trona-Wildrose Road, Panamint Valley Road, Highway 190, west to Panamint Springs Resort, Highway 136 to Highway 395.
ATTRACTIONS:
Trona (Gas, food, lodging supplies), **Trona Pinnacles, *Ballarat Ghost Town & Camp Ground, Panamint Valley, *Death Valley National Park, Panamint Springs Resort,* (Gas, food, lodging) **Darwin Falls, Rainbow Canyon, Keeler, *Cerro Gordo ghost town & mine, Keeler, Swansea.*
(*Indicates SIDE TRIPS from LOOP TRIP).
Return point to Highway 395 is at Interagency Visitor's Center 2 miles south of Lone Pine.
SERVICES ON ROUTE TRIP
Gas, food & lodging (Trona & Panamint Springs Resort) Camping (Ballarat & Panamint Springs Resort

SIDE TRIP TO CERRO GORDO EAST SIDE OF MONO LAKE
This side trip is described in detail on page 36
Right, east, on Hwy. 190 at the junction of Hwy 395, travels the southern side of Owens Lake.
ATTRACTIONS
Access to **Dirty Socks Hot Springs,*
Joins loop side trip "B' on Page at Hwy 136. **Cerro Gordo ghost town & mine, Keeler and Swansea.* Also gives access to Death Valley National Park, Panamint Valley by going right, south at Junction of Highways 190 & 136.
(*Indicates SIDE TRIPS from LOOP TRIP)
returns to Hwy 395 (34 miles total), 2 miles south of Lone Pine
NO SERVICES IN ROUTE

HIGHWAY 395, SECTION ONE
1-15, AT HESPERIA TO INDEPENDENCE

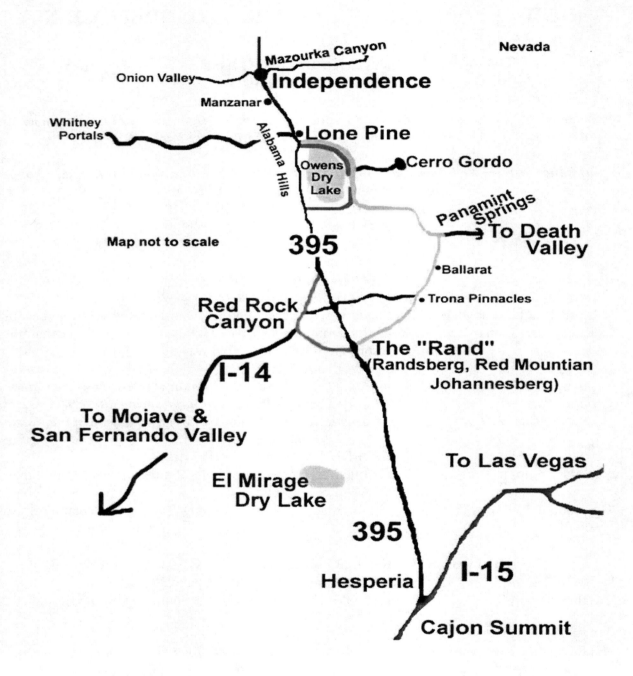

JUNCTION I-15 & 395
HESPERIA
MILE 0
Elevation 3,191'

Highway 395 from this point to the base of the Rand Mountains, 65 miles north, is relatively level with two lanes of traffic, one in each direction. Between this point and Kramer Junction, 42 miles, there can be a great deal of truck traffic, which generally reduces at the junction of Highway 58 at Kramer Junction.

HESPERIA
Gas, Food, Lodging, Full services

Located just north of the Cajon Summit, Hesperia became a stopping point for desert travelers as far back as the 1770's when the first known party of white men crossed the Mojave Desert.

As the trails from the east grew, so did the appeal of Hesperia.

The first known building in Hesperia was built in 1857. This hostelry was built by and operated by a journeyman named Hanbrier.

In 1847 the first railroad came to Hesperia. Hesperia was given its name when the railroad depot was completed and the area was officially named Hesperia

DOBY CORNERS
(Junction S.R. 18, Pearblossom/Palmdale Highway)
Gas, mini-mart
MILE 7
Victorville 4.8 miles east (All services)

ADELANTO
All Services
MILE 11
Elevation 2,877'
El Mirage Dry Lake, (BLM Barstow) 9 miles west on El Mirage Road

El Mirage Dry Lake first became popular during the 1930's when the flat dry lake was used by a group of land speed racers as a high-speed timing track. That original group, now known as the Southern California Timing Association, is still one of the groups using the dry lake today.

Two of the slower vehicles at El Mirage dry lake. The lake is seen in the background

Today this recreational area offers opportunities for land sailors, para-sails, kites, ultra lights, gyrocopter, model and full-sized airplanes and model rockets. There are camping areas sites for OHV enthusiasts in a special area of this recreation area.

El Mirage is divided into four general areas: dry lakebed, the basin, Shadow Mountains and Twin Hills.

The Bureau of Land Management in conjunction with other governmental entities administers the El Mirage Recreation Area.

GETTING THERE: In Adelanto take Crippen Avenue west from Highway 395 and follow the signs to Mountain View Road, which goes north and enters the recreational area. Information: BLM, 2601 Barstow Road, Barstow, CA. 92311, (760) 252-6098, www.elmirage.org/visitorinfo.htm

SHADOW MOUNTAIN ROAD
MILE 21
Access to *National Trails Highway (Route 66)*, 7 miles east at Silver Lakes
Shadow Mountain Road gives access to *Route 66* approximately mid-way between *Victorville* (south) and *Barstow* (north)

KRAMER JUNCTION
Junction Highway 58 (Four Corners)
Gas, food, Mini-mart, lodging
MILE 42
Elevation 2,500'
Town of *Boron*, 5 miles west (*20 Mule Team Museum*)
Full services
Mojave 37 miles west
Full Services
Barstow 33 miles east (note new cutoff to *Lenwood*, south of *Barstow*.)
Full services

Kramer Junction was for many years, and still is to a lesser degree today, a major railroad junction. In earlier days it was the 20 mule team borax wagons from Death Valley, then the trains coming south from Randsburg and out of the Owens Valley bearing gold now it is the borax from the mine at Boron coming to the junction to link up with the Southern Pacific Railroad's main line.

"THE RAND"
RED MOUNTAIN, RANDSBURG, JOHANNESBURG
MILE 69
Elevation 3,500'
Supplies, food, lodging, museum (Randsburg) lodging (Randsburg & Red Mountain)

The Desert Museum located on Butte Street, Randsburg

This entire area abounds with remnants of the past. Many of the original buildings and mine structures are found throughout the area.

This area has been mined for gold, silver and other precious metals for over a hundred years. While most of the medium sized operations are gone, the giant Yellow Aster/ Rand Mine and numerous individual mining operations are still taking gold out of the ground in this area.

Historic *Randsburg* is located 1 mile west of Highway 395 on the west side of the mountain from Red Mountain. All three of these historic communities reflect the past and offer numerous opportunities for both sign seers and antique shoppers. There is still gold panning done in the hills.

Randsburg is the largest of the communities and offers the most services.

At this writing, no gas is available in the area.

Life for Randsburg and Red Mountain began in 1895 when gold was discovered at the site of what was to become the Yellow Aster, or Rand Mine. The Yellow Aster/Rand Mine is still in operation today, providing income through employment and services for many of the residents of the three towns in this area.

Inside the historic Randsburg General Store

The town of Johannesburg, located 2 miles north of Red Mountain, was founded the following year, 1896, primarily as supply center for the mining operations in the area. It was in 1919 that silver was discovered in what is now Red Mountain. Initially Red Mountain was known as Osdick. California Land Mark #938 "Rand Mining District" is located in Randsburg.

In 1897 construction began on the Randsburg Railway. When service began in 1898 the line ran from Johannesburg south, 28 miles to Kramer, thus giving access to the Santa Fe Railroad main line. No, the line never got to Randsburg, its namesake. At the time of the construction of the railroad, the Yellow Aster mine was the largest gold mine in southern California. Operation of the railroad ceased in 1933.

The museum located on Butte Street, THE main street in Randsburg, is open weekends and holiday weekends from 10 am to 5 pm and contains much of the history of the area.

One of the "don't miss" attractions in Randsburg is the historic Randsburg General Store, 38 Butte Street. Constructed in 1896 the marble-topped fountain counter came around the "Horn" in the 1890's. One of the features of the historic fountain are the "made to order from syrup cokes" found here.

In addition to food and general merchandise the store offers numerous books, maps and information on the area.

THE HISTORIC COTTAGE HOTEL, TEA ROOM & GIFT SHOP

A "long block" east of the center of Randsburg is located a place where east truly does meet west. The Cottage Hotel features not only a bed and breakfast; complete with gifts and antiques, but it is also the location of "Granny Pat's Tea House." "A little taste of England in the middle of the desert" is how the owner operators of this interesting and delightful center put it.

Located at 130 Butte Avenue, reservations and information may be obtained by calling (760) 374-2285 or (888) COT HOBB or by writing Tobey Enterprises, P.O. Box 345, Randsburg, CA 93554. Website: www.randsburg.com, E-Mail Patfromafrica@direcway.

There are many historic attractions and interesting people to be found in the "Rand."

Remnants of a mineshaft head frame found outside of Red Mountain represent the "Rand's" historic past

LOOP SIDE TRIP "A"
This side trip is described in detail on Page 20.
Randsburg/Redrock Canyon Road from Randsburg, access to *Highway 14*, 21 miles, at a location 4 miles south of *Red Rock Canyon State Park*.
Return point to Highway 395, junctions Highways 14 and 395 west of Inyokern

ATTRACTIONS:
*Jawbone Canyon, Red Rock Canyon State Park, *Burro Schmidt's famous tunnel, *Robbers Roost, *Highway 178 access to **Lake Isabella,**
(*Indicates SIDE TRIPS from LOOP TRIP).
SERVICES ON ROUTE TRIP
Camping

LOOP SIDE TRIP "B"
This side trip is described in detail on Page 26.
Trona Road just south of Red Mountain gives access northeastward to Highway 178, east of Ridgecrest, Trona-Wildrose Road, Panamint Valley Road, Highway 190, (East into Death Valley National Park) west to Panamint Springs Resort, Highway 136 to Highway 395.

ATTRACTIONS:
Trona (Gas, food, lodging supplies), **Trona Pinnacles, *Ballarat Ghost Town & Camp Ground, Panamint Valley, *Death Valley National Park, Panamint Springs Resort,* (Gas, food, lodging) ***Darwin Falls, Rainbow Canyon, Keeler, *Cerro Gordo ghost town & Mine, Keeler, Swansea.**
(*Indicates SIDE TRIPS from LOOP TRIP).
Return point to Highway 395 is at Interagency Visitor's Center 2 miles south of Lone Pine.

SERVICES ON ROUTE TRIP
Gas, food & lodging (Trona & Panamint Springs Resort) Camping (Ballarat & Panamint Springs Resort
*

Leaving Rand Mountain Highway 395 is still two lanes and drops into the northern end of Fremont Valley and then climbs the southern side of the El Paso Mountains before dropping into Indian Wells Valley. These "ups and downs" are not particularly steep with the exception of a portion of the grade going up the El Paso Mountains where passing lanes are provided.

CHINA LAKE ROAD
MILE 109
Access to *Ridgecrest* and *China Lake*

RIDGECREST
Elevation 2,700'
Full Services *Maturango Museum*

The city of Ridgecrest offers full services, as does China Lake. The main attraction for many travelers however, is the Maturango Museum.

The Maturango Museum in addition to offering displays, exhibits and information on local history, offers tours of historic sites throughout the area including trips to petroglyphs located on the Navy's China Lake Naval Air Station.

Maturango Museum is located at 100 East Las Flores Avenue, one block north of Highway 178 east of Highway 395 (Business.) (760) 375-6900. Open everyday but holidays from 10 to 5. www.maturango.org

Ridgecrest Chamber of Commerce; 128 E. California Suite B. Ridgecrest, CA. 93556 (619) 375-8331

CHINA LAKE NAVAL AIR WEAPONS CENTER

Since 1943 the China Lake Naval Facility has been used as a research and test center for a variety of weapons. Today the center is used primarily for research and testing of naval aircraft weapons and missiles.

Encompassing over a million acres of the Mojave Desert many top-secret things pass through the air here.

Many of the ex-secret devices spanning four decades of testing are on display at the U. S. Naval Museum of Armament and Technology 1 Pearl Harbor Drive (end of Bundy St.) Open Monday through Friday, 9 am – 4 pm. (760) 939-3530.

INYOKERN ROAD (Highway 178)
MILE 118
Access to Inyokern & State Route 14 SOUTH (S.R.14 NORTH is 5 miles straight ahead)

JUNCTION STATE ROUTE 14
MILE 123

From this point northward through the Owens Valley and beyond, Highway 395 is a combination of both two and four lane roadway, divided in many places. Between here and Bishop the increase in altitude is quite gradual and generally not a factor in driving.

As an important note: during our travels up and down Highway 395 we have seen an unusually large number of motorists receiving what appeared to be speeding citations in the small towns along the highway. In most instances the speed limit is 25 MPH in these towns.

THE OWENS VALLEY

The area just north of the junction of Highways 395 and I-14 commonly considered to be the beginning of the 145-mile long Owens Valley, which extends northward to just above Bishop.

This valley has seen everything from Indian wars to water wars, and while invaded in the winter by skiers and other winter sports enthusiasts and in the summer by campers, fishermen, hikers, tourist sightseers and other travelers, it has lost none of its appeal.

For centuries the Native Americans had both lived in and traveled through this valley, oft-times seeking refuge from the mountains which surrounded it and on other occasions seeking game and other foodstuffs.

In 1859 the Indian wars broke out in the Owens Valley. As a result the Army opened Fort Independence on July 4, 1852, hence the area to become the town of Independence gained its name.

In 1862 at what became known as The Battle of Bishop, approximately 50 settlers and 500 Indians fought. In all over 200 Native Americans were killed in battles with the settlers.

Various trappers and hunters had used the valley as a source for game. It was 1861 before the first structure of a permanent nature was built in the north end of the valley. The first settlement was called Owensville. At about this same time the Putnam Residence in Independence was built.

Gold was the initial calling for most of those who arrived in the Owens Valley in those earlier days.

Soon ranchers began moving cattle and sheep into the valleys. Farmers followed also taking advantage of the plentiful water and good soil.

Beginning in 1905 a different type of warfare broke out in the Owens Valley.

The city of Los Angeles required new sources of water for its staggering growth so, the city of Los Angeles came to Owens Valley to get it. Water rights and various parcels of land were acquired by the city.

In 1907 an aqueduct began construction to carry the water to Los Angeles. The Owens River water in addition to the water from streams further north was diverted.

The ranchers and farmers of the Owens Valley begin to disappear. Soon Owens Lake, once the home to steamboats, did disappear. The fruit orchards, farms and ranches of the Owens Valley dried up, and died.

Bordered on the west by the majestic Sierra Nevada Mountains and on the east by the White and the Inyo Mountains, the valley gives access to numerous attractions.

PEARSONVILLE
Gas, mini-mart, raceway, hubcap capital of Highway 395
MILE 131
Elevation 2,470'

JUNCTION STATE ROUTE 141 (NINE MILE ROAD/KENNEDY MEADOWS ROAD)
Mile 134
(CLOSED IN WINTER)
Access via Sherman Pass to Kennedy Meadows, 26 miles, Kernville/Lake Isabella 103 Miles.

LITTLE LAKE
West, NO Services
Mile 140

"Shake and bake" is an excellent name for this abandoned town. Between here and Coso, to the north, there are "swarms" of earthquakes reported on a regular basis.

Long a stopping place along the highway, once known as "Little Owens Lake," this picturesque spot sported good food, water for boiling radiators and a comfortable hotel for the traveler

Little Lake is now a ghost town. The Little Lake Hotel, which opened in 1923, after standing for years in ruins and fire damage, is totally gone now.

The lake itself, located on the east side of the highway, can be quite spectacular as the black lava formations and the green reeds frame it.

FOSSIL FALLS *(BLM- RIDGECREST)*
Cinder Road - East (Just south of the large cinder mountain on the right)
Mile 143

The large amount of lava seen along the east side of the highway can be studied first hand at this spot.

The earth has been busy through the ages in this area as evidenced by the remnants of volcanic activity found here at Fossil Falls. As recently as 20,000 years ago lava from local volcanic eruptions flowed into the area. The action of the Owens River sculptured the lava into the varied forms which may be observed at Fossil Falls today.

From 4000 BC until European contact in the 19th century the Little Lake Shoshone Indians inhabited the area. Much evidence of this has been found in the area in the form of art and utensils. Please let these remnants of the past continue to be a testament to the past by leaving them undisturbed! Besides, collecting the artifacts is a felony.

The "falls" of Fossil Falls are located on a one half mile round-trip trail from the parking lot. The trail to the falls is quite as easy one.

Scaling the falls should be left to the experts with the proper equipment.

COSO JUNCTION
East
Cal-Trans rest area *(Eastern Sierra Byway Location)*
Gas, Fast food, market/general store
Mile 148

For years the historic town of Coso, located to the east of the present Coso, was a crossroads for the travelers from the east and from the north and south.

More recently both the locals and the travelers used the Coso Hot Springs to relieve their aches and pains.

Today, the historic ghost town of Coso lies behind locked gates along with the once famous Coso Hot Springs. Now a part of the China Lake Naval Air Station these historic spots are accessible via guided tours through the Maturango Museum in Ridgecrest.

Everyone we have met working in the Coso Junction Store, so far, has been "local" and had a wealth of information on the area which they were willing to share.

OLANCHA
Gas, Food & Lodging
Mile 165

This small community is basically a crossroads for Highway 190 and a source of supplies for locals and travelers. Good Food

JUNCTION HIGHWAY 190
SIDE TRIP TO DIRTY SOCKS HOT SPRINGS & CERRO GORDO
Mile 166
Described on page 36.
East Access to Highway136/190, 15 miles

East from the junction of Hwy 190 it is 31 miles to Panamint Springs Resort, 61 Miles to Stovepipe Wells, Death Valley

Going right, east, at the junction of Hwys. 190 & 395 travels along the southern side of Mono Lake. Access to *Dirty Socks Hot Springs.* At the junction of Hwys 190 & 136, mile 15, the route joins loop trip "B", page 33, with access to *Cerro Gordo*, *Keeler and Swansea* returns to Hwy 395 at the Interagency Visitors Center, 2 miles south of Lone Pine (34 miles total.)

OWENS LAKE

For the next 18 miles we will be traveling along the western shore of what is now the dried remains of Owens Lake. The prime reason the lake is now "dead" is that the Los Angeles Department of Water and Power acquired the water rights in the area as water supply for the city.

As we look across the expanse of this now dead lake toward the Inyo Mountains on the eastern shore, it is hard to picture the steamboats which used to travel the lake's length. Owens Lake once gave passage to steamboats carrying ore from the mines located on the northeastern side of the lake to a port located at Olancha where the boats were reloaded with supplies and workers and headed back across the lake.

About the only thing that crossed Owens Lake on this day was a dust storm. The Los Angeles Department of Water and power is now using water sprinklers and plants to cut the dust down

COTTONWOOD CHARCOAL KILNS
East
Mile 174

The two historic kilns are located about a mile east of the highway. (The access road to the kilns CAN BE quite soft and hazardous for two wheel drive vehicles, you may wish to park and walk the last part of the way.)

These beehive shaped kilns were used to create charcoal bricks which were used in silver-mine smelters during the 19th century.

The wood for the kilns was sent down the mountainside in "V" shaped flumes. Much of the charcoal was shipped across Owens Lake by steamboat, while some of it was hauled to the smelters by wagons.

While there has been some vandalism to the kilns, it is not hard to visualize the blazing fires within them, turning the wood into charcoal.

JUNCTION HIGHWAY 136
INTERAGENCY VISITOR'S CENTER *(Eastern Sierra Scenic Site)*
East
Mile 188
Open Daily (Closed Jan.1, Thanksgiving, Dec.25)
This multi-agency center offers the visitor/traveler information from many sources.

Guides, maps, books, special flyers, exhibits and information from the center's attendants offer a real look into the area and its multitude of attractions.

Information on everything from Mount Whitney and the Sierra Nevada Mountains, to the attractions found throughout the Owens Valley to Death Valley is found here. Eastern Sierra InterAgency Visitor Center, P.O. Box R, Lone Pine, CA 93545, (760) 876-6222

The Interagency visitor's center with its High Sierras backdrop

Highway 136 gives access along the north side of Owens to Swansea, Keeler and Cerro Gordo. Further east is access into Panamint Valley and Death Valley, in a loop route described on page 26.

CITY OF LONE PINE
Full Services
Mile 191
Elevation 3,700'

Looming over Lone Pine to the west is one of the tallest sections of the Eastern High Sierra Mountain Range, including the tallest mountain in the continental United States, Mount Whitney.

In 1879 an earthquake of a magnitude of 8.5+, all but leveled the town of Lone Pine and killed 29 of the town's residents. The only remnant of the pre-1879 town is a portion of a wall located on Main Street. The cemetery where the earthquake victims are buried is located just north of town on the west side of the highway and is marked by California State Landmark #507.

Much of the recent history of Lone Pine is the result of the motion pictures that have been filmed there. Many of the restaurants and shops contain memories of the stars and the movies in which they appeared. Pictures adorn the walls and several books on the movie history of the area are to be found in many of the gift shops found throughout Lone Pine.

A winter storm rages in the Sierras, high above the sun covered roofs of downtown Lone Pine

Every year on Columbus Day Weekend there is a Film Festival held in Lone Pine in the commemoration of the filming done in the area. Information on current festivals may be obtained through the Lone Pine Chamber of Commerce.

LONE PINE CHAMBER OF COMMERCE
120 S. MAIN ST (P.O. BOX 749)
LONE PINE, CA. 93545
(760) 876-4444

Lone Pine offers a wide variety of eateries, from fast food to restaurants and a dinner house. Numerous hotels and motels in addition to campsites, located to the south and primarily to the west of town, are found in the Lone Pine area.

Both lake and stream fishing are found in the waters surrounding Lone Pine.

POINTS OF INTEREST FOUND WEST OF LONE PINE
ALABAMA HILLS, WHITNEY PORTALS
West at the stoplight at Highway 395 & Whitney Portal Road.

ALABAMA HILLS
Movie Road, RIGHT (2 ½ miles west of Highway 395)

Over 450 motion pictures in addition to numerous television shows and commercials have been filmed in the hills located to the west of Lone Pine. These unusual formations, found in the Alabama Hills, have seen the filming of everything from Gunga Din to dozens of Hopalong Cassidy films and The Great Race among many others.

Named for a Civil War battleship these mountains present an entirely different look on their western side than they do on the side facing Highway 395.

WHITNEY PORTAL
Elevation 8,371'
Camping, fishing, hiking, supplies, sandwiches

Thirteen miles west of the town of Lone Pine is Whitney Portals, the access point to Mount Whitney. Much of the roadway to Whitney Portals, before it was paved, can be seen in the 1941 Humphrey Bogart classic film, "High Sierra."

This view from Whitney Portal Road shows the roadway as it passes the Alabama Hills (center of photo) following Lone Pine Creek (the dark area paralleling the roadway.) The patch of dark between the hills is the town of Lone Pine. The dark line running behind the Alabama Hills is the Owens riverbed. The Owens Valley and the Inyo Mountains form the background

Lone Pine Creek cascades down the mountainside and under a wooden bridge. A picnic area, trout pond gift shop and restaurant await the traveler while several campgrounds are at this 8,371-foot high hideaway.

Whitney Portal is also the most popular jumping off spot for those who desire to climb the 14,494-foot high Mount Whitney. The peak is reached via a 10.7-mile trail. One must have a permit in order to climb Mount Whitney, or even to be on the trail overnight. Information on Mount Whitney climbing permits, which have been done by lottery in the past, or on the overnight trail permits, may be obtained from the Mt. Whitney Ranger District, P.O. Box 8, Lone Pine, CA 93545, (760) 876-6200. www.nps.gov/seki/whitney.htm.

Map reprinted courtesy of National Park Service, 2001

MANZANAR NATIONAL HISTORIC SITE *(Eastern Sierra Byway Site)*
(National Park Service)
Mile 199
West
No facilities or services

While the best-known history of Manzanar is its most recent, it has long been a center for the people of Owens Valley.

For centuries this area was used by the Owens Valley Paiutes as evidenced by the artifacts and archeological sites found in the area.

From 1910 until the mid-1930's an agricultural village known as Manzanar, a thriving pear and apple-growing center was located here.

Many of the prior residents visit the site.

Today this military guard station marks the entrance to The Manzanar National Historic Site

From 1942 to 1945 this was the site of an internment camp for over 10,000 Japanese-Americans.

The detention facility encompassed some 6,000 acres and contained virtually of the amenities required of any community of that size. Agricultural areas, sewage treatment facilities, a cemetery and even an airport made up the Manzanar of the early 1940's.

Plans are in the works to restore the large building to the northeast from the gate which was used as the auditorium during the 1940's. Plans are that this building is to be used as a combination Visitor Center and Park Headquarters.

Other plans include the reconstruction of one guard tower, barracks and internee built gardens.

With the exception of the guard station and cement foundations, little remains of the historic relocation center. Or was it a concentration camp? People will be arguing this point for years.

Self-guided auto and walking tour guides and general information brochures are available from the box located on the north side at the first guard kiosk at the entrance. Additional information is available at the Eastern California Museum located to the north in Independence.

For additional information contact the National Park Service, Manzanar National Historic Site, P.O. Box 426, Independence, CA 93526-0426, (760) 878-2194.

INDEPENDENCE
Mile 207
Gas, Food, Lodging, *Eastern California Museum*
Elevation 3,925'

Since 1866 this sleepy little town has been the county seat of sprawling Inyo County.

The town's history begins in August of 1861when Charles Putnam built the first permanent cabin just west of what is now Highway 395 (California Historic Marker # 223 at 135 Edwards Street.) On July 4, 1862 a military post was established here along the banks of the Owens River, hence the name "Independence." (California Historic Marker #349.) See Mount Whitney Fish Hatchery for location on both commander's residence and the location of the original Fort Independence.

The area has hosted gold miners, railroad builders, farmers, movie pioneers, and cattle ranchers as well as the army post.

While no gold was found in the area it did become the location of ranches and became a supply center. The addition of a narrow gauge railroad in 1883 hastened the growth of the area.

There are numerous historic points of interest to be found in the Independence area.

The Mary Austin Home, California Historic Landmark # 229 is located on Market Street 2 blocks west of Highway 395 and one block east of the Eastern California Museum.

EASTERN CALIFORNIA MUSEUM, 155 North Grant Street (take Market Street 3 blocks west from Highway 395) Since 1928 this museum has featured a growing number of exhibits which reflects the diverse natural and cultural heritage of Inyo County.

The museum contains extensive information on the history of Manzanar in addition to numerous other features of the county

The Eastern California Museum contains an extensive
Collection of information, including numerous artifacts

In addition to the constantly increasing number of exhibits found inside the museum, the grounds around the museum are filled with buildings and implements depicting more of the history of the area.

The museum is open Wed – Sun. with the exception of major holidays. Information: (760) 878-0364.

FORT INDEPENDENCE COMMANDER'S HOUSE is located across the street from the Masonic Hall, at the corner of Highway 395 and Main Street in Independence. Built between 1886 and 1890, this is one of the few remaining examples of Victorian architecture in Owens Valley. Built of lumber believed to have been recycled from Camp Independence this historic Victorian home is open a few times a year. Contact the Eastern California Museum for information.

ONION VALLEY is located 14 miles west of Independence off of Market Street that becomes Onion Valley Road, just west of Independence. The side trip to Onion Valley side trip is found on Page 37.

KEARSARGE AND MAZOURKA CANYON The abandoned site of the town of *Kearsarge* (named for the Civil War ship) is found 5 miles east of Highway 395 along Mazourka Canyon Road. The foundations of this old mining town give an insight into its layout.

It is interesting to note that the town of *Kearsarge,* the name of a northern ship, was so named by Yankee Civil War vets in "retaliation" for the naming of the *Alabama Hills* by the southern sympathizers in the area.

Continuing west and north along *Mazourka Canyon Road* **(RV ALERT: The road past Kearsarge is gravel, quite steep and could be hazardous in a vehicle not designed for such travel.)** As the roadway climbs its way up the Inyo Mountains more and more abandoned mines and mine shafts dot the area.

Along Mazurka Canyon Road, Owens Valley and the High Sierras form the backdrop.

Some 8 miles up the canyon there is a well-traveled road to the left, west. Some 2 miles up this road you will enter 4 WD country and encounter a road to the right. This road is *actually* a loop. About ¾ of the way up the hill you will be treated to a magnificent view of Owens Valley, all of the way to Lone Pine, Mount Whitney and beyond.

AT INDEPENDENCE RESET MILEAGE TO 0

The following section contains detail descriptions the 2 loop trips and 2 side trips, which are a part of this section.

LOOP SIDE TRIP "A"
Randsburg Redrock Canyon Road from Randsburg, access to *Highway 14*, 21 miles, at a location
5 miles south of *Red Rock Canyon State Park.*
Return point to Highway 395, junction Highway 14 northwest of Inyokern
50 Miles to return point with Highway 395 TAKING LOOP TRIP
31 Miles to return point with Highway 395 by NOT TAKING LOOP TRIP
ATTRACTIONS:
*Jawbone Canyon, Red Rock Canyon State Park, *Burro Schmidt's famous tunnel, *Robbers Roost, *Highway 178 access to Lake Isabella,*
(*Indicates SIDE TRIPS from LOOP TRIP).
SERVICES AVAILABLE
Jawbone Canyon, Red Rock Canyon; Camping, chemical toilets
Full Services and supplies; Inyokern

PLEASE NOTE: Much of the material included in this "loop trip" is taken directly from the authors publications "Windshield Adventuring Through the Mojave Desert" ISBN# 0-9664055-1-X and "Mojave Desert Windshield Adventures" ISBN# 0-9664055-8-7

RANDSBURG MILE 0

From the west end of Butte Avenue, the main drag of Randsburg, go west on *Red Rock Randsburg Road.* Eight and one half miles west of Randsburg is the intersection of *Garlock Road.* Continue westward on *Red Rock Randsburg Road.* (Just to the east of the intersection are the remnants of the town of Garlock. A plaque marks the location which includes the fenced ruins of several historic buildings.)

JUNCTION HIGHWAY 14
Mile 21

Highway 14 is an alternate route to the eastern Sierra, joining Highway 395 at Inyo Kern. Many travelers use this route as there is more four-lane road to the south than is found on Highway 395. Portions of Highway 14 between this point and the junction with Highway 395 are also four lane.

MILEAGE SHOWN HERE STARTS AGAIN AT ZERO (0)

JAWBONE STATION BLM INFORMATION CENTER
2 Miles <u>SOUTH</u> of *Red Rock Canyon Randsburg Road*
No food or gasoline chemical toilets

Two miles to the south of the junction of Red Rock Canyon/Randsburg Road and Highways 395 is the BLM's Jawbone Canyon Station. While the Jawbone Canyon area is primarily used by off-roaders, the information center offers a rather complete selection of maps, books and information on the entire area. The information center is open seven days a week, excluding major holidays. (760) 373-1146.

The town of Mojave (full services) is 18 miles south of Jawbone Station on Highway 14.

GOING **NORTH** ON HIGHWAY 14: (from Red Rock Canyon/Randsburg Road)

RED ROCK CANYON STATE PARK & CAMPGROUND
5 Miles north of Red Rock Randsburg Road

Much of the beauty of this park is available as you drive through it at 55 M.P.H. on the divided highway that literally splits the park in two.

The ever-changing colors of the magnificent formations offer beauty and uniqueness, which draws numerous hikers, campers, geologists, paleontologists and moviemakers to this site. The sculptured sandstone cliffs with their whites, pinks, reds and blacks and seem to be almost from another planet.

Red Cliffs National Preserve, Red Rock Canyon

In the spring, with sufficient rainfall during the winter months, the area will abound with the additional colors of numerous varieties of wild flowers. In addition to the wild flowers there are numerous varieties of plants and wild life here in the park. One of the major nesting areas for eagles, hawks, owls and falcons is located within the park. It is not unusual to see these large birds of prey riding the thermal updrafts in their search for food. The park offers a multitude of hiking trails and an abundance of roads.

GETTING THERE: This State Park straddles State Highway 14 just 5 miles north of the intersection of *Red Rock-Randsburg Road* intersection and is 24 miles north of the city of Mojave.

CAMPSITE FEATURES: State Park, 50 campsites, trailer/RV (no hookups) dump station available, fee. Moderate privacy, pit toilets, potable water, and no showers. Located in a beautiful location beneath sandstone cliffs. Red Rock Canyon Park has a ranger station with full time staff & ranger residing in the park. Camping fee. Elevation: 2,700 feet. No reservations.

SERVICES: Firewood for sale at visitor center in the park. Cafe, groceries, and lodging are available at Randsburg, 25 miles east of the park or in Mojave. Complete services are also available at Inyokern and Ridgecrest. The visitor center/ranger station features exhibits, maps & books plus information on the general area, not just limited to the park. All of the personnel were not only friendly but also quite knowledgeable on the entire area.

Additionally, there are periodically scheduled talks and hikes by the ranger. At the southern end of the campground is an excellent self-guiding wilderness trail. An extension of the trail of about a 1/4 of a mile will take the hiker across several ridges and afford a dramatic view.

Within the park there are several dirt roads that can afford additional sightseeing. *WARNING:* CHECK WITH THE PARK RANGERS BEFORE TAKING SIDE ROADS! Some of the roads can be impassable even with a 4-wheel drive vehicle

The September 1988 flood created extensive damage to the facilities (all repaired now) but left spectacular damage in its wake, which can be seen throughout the central portion of the park. *Information:* (760) 942-0662, www.calparksmojave.com/redrocks/

RED ROCK – INYOKERN ROAD
ACCESS TO EL PASO MOUNTAINS AND BURROW SCHMIDT'S TUNNEL
Mile 7.5

Stretching eastward from Red Rock Canyon State Park, the El Paso Mountains are riddled with almost as much history as they are old tunnels and mine shafts.

Nearby Points Of Interest: Exploring The El Paso Mountains. Burro Schmidt's Famous Tunnel, Opal Mining (Do It Yourself In The Tailings!).

BURROW SCHMIDT'S INFAMOUS TUNNEL

"We took off to see Schmidt's Tunnel which is northeast from Red Rock Canyon in the El Paso Mountains. The country is beautiful and the lady who lives there, Toni Seger, has been there for 40 years. Her husband needed dry air after the Korean War so she bought this property out in the middle of the desert. She came up here to buy in the late 50's and said she probably would not have ended up where she did except the real estate man tried to tell her that she didn't want "that" piece of property. She says that you should never tell a Vermont Yankee what he does or doesn't want. She had a brand new car, a poodle with a pom-pom haircut, three-inch heels, a hat, white gloves and a suit while everyone else was wearing dungarees. But she got the property. Her husband died a year or so after that but she's been here ever since. There is a black cat to keep her company and she says she's on her 6th Jeep but she's pretty content. Burro Schmidt built himself the "registration" shed he. The roof inside is "insulated" with old magazines like Collier's and Saturday Evening Posts and old newspapers. (I spotted one with what looked like a very young Carole Lombard as a "starlet whose beauty the photographer has just captured.") On the way out, Toni showed me what turned out to be covered over steps right by the front door that lead to the cellar. Toni has asthma and bronchitis and it's not sure how long she'll be able to live up on her hill. (She has mentioned her family wasn't happy with her being alone out there) but it is a real treat to meet a lady like her and to see an old piece of desert history, to wit: Schmidt's Tunnel. Seems that Mr. Schmidt got the idea that a tunnel through the mountain would make taking ore from his claim and others on that side of the mountains easier than hauling it all the way around. Thirty-eight years later, he made it

through. The only tools he used were a six-pound maul, chisels, a mine cart, and two mules. The mules are what got him his nickname of Burro Schmidt. The tunnel is a half-mile long and for most of its length, I had no trouble standing up. Russ didn't do as well. He had to be careful or else get clobbered. The funny part is that it runs straight for most of its length then makes a 90^0, right hand turn for the last part. I can't figure how he knew to make the turn <u>right there.</u> It also shows that he was getting tired because this part of the tunnel is where even I had to duck my head. The whole section is shorter. The worst part is that 10-12 years into this 38-year project, a railroad spur had been put into the valley and meant that the tunnel wasn't needed. He just wouldn't give up his idea. The view one the other side is spectacular. You can walk back over the top of the hill but it is steep and windy climb so we came back through the tunnel."

Kathy Spencer

GETTING THERE: In addition to access via the map below, there is access some 7 miles north of the junction of Highway 395 and Red Rock/Inyo Kern Road via a signed road.

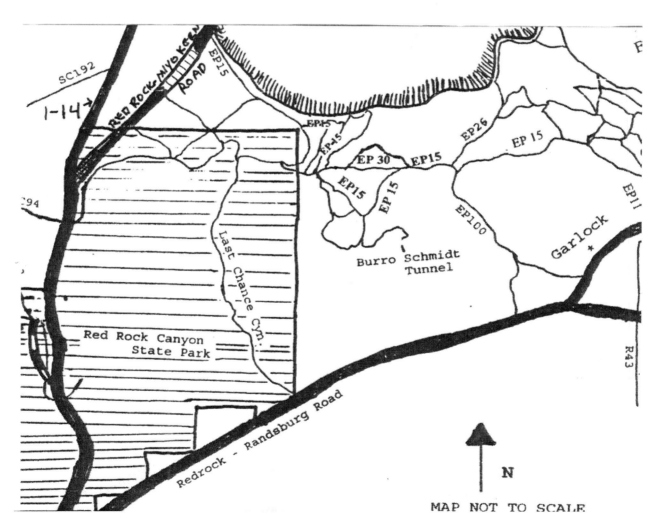

MAP COURTESY BLM (APRIL 1999)

BURROW SCHMIDT'S TUNNEL ACCESS
Mile 15.1
Additional access to that via *Red Rock - Inyo Kern Road*

ROBBERS ROOST ACCESS
Mile 18.5

At the time of this writing there is an abandoned store/service station marking the turn onto BLM roadway marked "SC333".

ROBBERS' ROOST

This outcropping, which looks out across the Indian Hills Valley, was often used as a hideout for marauding Indians and bandits, including the famous Tiburcio Vasquez. These 19th century scoundrels preyed upon the wagon trains and other settlers on their way westward from Death Valley to Walker Pass, which lays some 6 miles up Freeman Canyon, now Highway 178, just a mile north of this rocky hideout.

The view from these giant granite monoliths eliminates any questions as to why, in addition to caves and crags to hide in, bandits and marauding Indians laid in wait for victims here.

Robbers' Roost is now used primarily as a nesting site for, birds of prey instead of people of prey. In fact the site is closed to all vehicular traffic from February 1 through July 1 to protect the nesting of the red tail hawk, prairie falcon and other raptors that nest in the rocky crags and caves.

Looking like giant sentinels, these monoliths are 2 miles west of Highway 14 and 1 mile south of Highway 178.

GETTING THERE: Area is CLOSED TO VEHICLES from FEBRUARY 1 TO JULY 1. Access by high clearance or 4 wheel drive vehicles. From Highway 178: 1 mile west of Highway 14 go south on BLM SC56 approximately one mile to BLM SC333 go west to location. From Highway

14 go west on BLM SC51, which is located at the north end of an abandoned commercial location.

HIGHWAY 178 WEST, ACCESS TO LAKE ISABELLA, BAKERSFIELD
Mile 23

The town of *Lake Isabella* is located over the Walker Pass and some 45 miles west of this junction at the western end of Lake Isabella. Walker Pass is named for Joseph R. Walker, American trailblazer, who came east through this pass from the San Joaquin Valley in 1834.

Your author, closest to camera in hat, rafting the Kern River south of Lake Isabella

HIGHWAY 178 EAST TO RIDGECREST & CHINA LAKE
Mile 26
Full Services, access to *Maturango Museum*

This is probably your best bet for services as the Junction point 3 miles north is remote from most services.

JUNCTION HIGHWAY 395, END OF HIGHWAY 14 & OF OUR LOOP TRIP
Mile 29

LOOP SIDE TRIP "B"

Trona Road just south of Red Mountain gives access northeastward to Highway 178, east of Ridgecrest, Trona-Wildrose Road, Panamint Valley Road, Highway 190, (East into Death Valley National Park) west to Panamint Springs Resort, Highway 136 to Highway 395.

ATTRACTIONS:

*Trona (Gas, food, lodging supplies), *Trona Pinnacles, *Ballarat Ghost Town & Camp Ground, Panamint Valley, *Death Valley National Park, Panamint Springs Resort, (Gas, food, lodging) *Darwin Falls, Rainbow Canyon, Keeler, *Cerro Gordo ghost town & Mine, Keeler, Swansea.*

(*Indicates SIDE TRIPS from LOOP TRIP).

Return point to Highway 395 is at Interagency Visitor's Center 2 miles south of Lone Pine.

137 Miles to return point with Highway 395 BY TAKING THE LOOP TRIP

119 Miles to return point with Highway 395 by NOT TAKING LOOP TRIP

SERVICES ON ROUTE TRIP

Gas, food & lodging (Trona & Panamint Springs Resort) Camping (Ballarat & Panamint Springs Resort)

PLEASE NOTE: Some of the material included in this "loop trip" is taken directly from the authors publications "Windshield Adventuring Through the Mojave Desert" ISBN# 0-9664055-1-X and "Mojave Desert Windshield Adventures" ISBN# 0-9664055-8-7

SET MILEAGE AT 0 IN RANDSBURG

The entire trip is on two-lane (one lane in each direction) maintained roads. There are fairly steep hills coming out of Panamint Valley in either direction. Large trucks may be encountered between Trona and Ballarat due to the mine located near Ballarat.

From Highway 395 go right, north, on Trona Road is approximately ½ mile north of Red Mountain or you can take the Searles Station Cut-off, which is 6 miles north east of Red Mountain. The two roads intersect northeast of Highway 395

The road climbs the Spangler Hills and then drops into the Searles Valley, which contains both the Trona Pinnacles and the town of Trona.

JUNCTION HIGHWAY 178
Mile 20

Turn right at the junction of Highway 178, the designation (but not the road) ends at the Trona Pinnacles turn off.

Seven miles east of the junction of Highway 178 is the access road to Trona Pinnacles Natural Landmark.

TRONA PINNACLES NATIONAL NATURAL LANDMARK
Mile 32.5 (access road, additional 7 miles to pinnacles)
NO SERVICES
Altitude 2,000'

The sight of some 500 tufa spires rising as high as 140 feet from the Searles Dry Lake basin can give the effect of suddenly arriving at some location in outer space. The folks who brought us numerous motion pictures, including "Star Trek V - The Final Frontier obviously thought so, as the area has been used to depict "outer space" in more than one adventure film.

These tufa (calcium carbonate) formations were formed between 10,000 and 100,000 years ago when Searles Lake was up to 640 feet deep. The pinnacles were formed underwater as the result of interaction of blue-green algae, local chemicals and geothermal conditions.

The pinnacles cover an area roughly 3 miles wide by 4.5 miles long.

There are NO FACILITIES at the pinnacles including NO REST ROOMS. Primitive camping is available at the Pinnacles in previously used areas and fire-rings. You must pack out all trash: LEAVE NO TRACE

Summer temperatures can reach over 120 degrees here making fall, winter and spring the best times to visit.

GETTING THERE: Located approximately 20 miles east of the city of Rosamond at the point where State Highway 178, east turns into a county road. The Pinnacles are located 7 miles south of the highway via a graded dirt road. This access road is usually passable by any passenger vehicle. If there has been a recent rain in the area it is advisable to check the road conditions with B.L.M. Ridgecrest Resource Area Office.

BLM Field Office, 300 South Richmond Blvd Ridgecrest, (760) 384-5400,
www.cablm.gov/caso/information.html

Past the Trona Pinnacles access road, we will lose the highway designation and the roadway eventually becomes *Trona Wildrose Road*, we will be passing Searles Dry Lake on the right.

TRONA
Mile 39,6
Gas, Food, lodging, all services (Next services are quite distant in any direction)
Elevation 1,659

Trona is one of those places in the world that exists for a specific purpose. Trona was conceived in 1872 when John Searles realized that the dried crystals he had discovered ten years earlier in the dried lake (subsequently named for him) were borax.

From that point in history on, Trona has been a busy place with a varied assortment of individuals and large companies mining the numerous materials found in Searles Dry Lake. Trona exists for mining. The California State Marker located in the rest area in town states that fully one half of the natural elements known to man are found here.

Borax, sodium sulfate, boric acid and soda ash are some of the products originating here.

Geologists report that the giant dry lake's evaporation left some three billion tons of soluble mineral salts. North American Chemical Company purchased all of the plants, operations, land, and leases for the Searles Dry Lakebed in 1990.

TRONA MUSEUM (OLD GUEST HOUSE MUSEUM)

This large well-organized and recently expanded museum gives a true insight into this interesting area from its early days through today. The museum is designed to show the visitor all facets of the area's history. The file room contains a wealth of research data. While there, don't miss the information on the monorail that was once used to transport raw materials to the mill. In addition to the museum, the Searles Valley Historical Society also offers the visitor the opportunity to visit the History House (one of Trona's oldest residences), the Trona Railway Museum and caboose at 83001 Panamint Street. The Society has plas to soon have two historic fire trucks on display. The History House and the Railway Museum are seen by appointment.

The Museum is open Monday, Wednesday, Thursday, and Saturday from 9 a.m. to noon and on Tuesday and Friday from 10 a.m. to 1 p.m. Other times are available by appointment only. The museum is located two blocks north of the county highway from the roadside rest area on Center Street. Go right on Main Street and one block to the parking lot.

Old Guest House Museum
13193 Main Street
Trona, Ca. 93592
Call (760) 372-4800
http://www1.iwvisp.com/svhs

From the town of Trona, the two-lane road continues to the Slate Range Pass, elevation 2,800', from where it drops into the southern end of Panamint Valley.

PANAMINT VALLEY

It was here that the ancient movements within the earth lay almost bare. The gold and other precious metals were shoved near the surface where 19th and 20th century prospectors and miners could harvest them.

It was in Panamint Valley that the half burnt travelers, the first to cross Death Valley, found water at a spring near what was later to become the mining town of Ballarat.

The mountain ranges on both sides of the valley became a beehive of mining activity, while some of these attempts at riches failed, many went on to become bonanzas. In fact one of these bonanzas is still in operation today, a few miles to the south of Ballarat.

The hills above Ballarat once alive with mining activity have many remains there today for those who would climb them. Emmett C. Harder's excellent book, "These Canyons are Full of Ghosts," The Last of the Death Valley Prospectors, tells tales of recent prospecting the area.

BALLARAT
Mile 63 (Ballarat Road, turn east 4 miles)
Elevation 1,087'
Camping, no services or supplies available

One of the historical buildings surrounding the campground at Ballarat

Located 3 1/2 miles east of Panamint Valley Road some 23 miles south of Highway 190 there is a commemorative marker and signs leading to the ghost town of Ballarat, which can be seen across *Panamint Dry Lake* at the base of the Panamint Mountains.

Named for a gold district in Australia, this town was founded in 1897 as a supply center for the mining communities located above the town in the Panamint Mountains. At the turn of the century *Ballarat* boasted a population of 400 people, a 2-story hotel, 7 saloons & 2 houses of ill repute. The former jail has been converted into a gift shop.

The wildlife in this area includes big horn sheep and wild burros. Occasionally, someone lures some of the wild burros out of the hills to eat food that has been left for them.

Today Ballarat is a camping/RV area located among some of the still standing adobe ruins of the original town. Camping here is primitive with no hookups. Showers are available at an additional charge. **BRING YOUR OWN DRINKING WATER YOU MAYBE UNABLE TO BUY IT THROUGHOUT THE ENTIRE VALLEY.** The water in the valley is not purified. **NO GAS, TELEPHONE OR ROOMS ARE AVAILABLE IN BALLARAT**.
www.fieler.com/ballarat/index.html

WILDROSE CANYON ROAD
LIMITED ACCESS (No vehicles over 25' long or 9' wide allowed)
Mile 71

Wildrose Canyon Road is, in spots, quite narrow with minimal side clearance and sharp curves. A vehicle with excessive length or side clearance is subject to becoming stuck.

While the attractions accessible from Wildrose Canyon Road are certainly interesting, it's a long way for a tow once you go up the canyon.

Access to Wildrose Charcoal Kilns, Eureka Mine/ Aguereberry Camp, Aguereberry Point, Stovepipe Wells Center, Death Valley National Park (full services).

Our road changes names here from *Trona-Wildrose Road* to *Panamint Valley Road*.

JUNCTION HIGHWAY 190
Mile 85
EAST, RIGHT TURN (not on our loop trip)
Stovepipe Wells, Death Valley National Park 28 Miles, all services.

Death Valley Information: Death Valley National Park, P.O. Box 579, Death Valley, CA 92328, (760) 786-2331 www.nps.gov/deva/

WEST, LEFT TURN
(Continues our loop trip back to Highway 395)

PANAMINT SPRINGS RESORT (2 ½ miles west of Panamint Valley Road)
Mile 87
Gas, food, supplies, camping, lodging

Panamint Springs over looks the northern end of The Panamint Valley and the Panamint Dunes from its location on the eastern slope of the Darwin Hills. Located mid-way between the town of Lone Pine and Stovepipe Wells in Death Valley National Park, Panamint Springs is a great jumping off place for adventures in the Panamint area.

Panamint Springs consists of a motel, campground/RV park, restaurant, mini mart and gas station. The motel rooms are small but clean with individual baths including showers.

After spending much time both in Death Valley itself and at Panamint Springs we feel that Panamint Springs is much cooler in summer that Death Valley. The temperature difference is due to the higher altitude of Panamint Springs. Panamint Springs also is cooler at night.

The stories of the actual springs at Panamint Springs vary, depending upon who tells the tale. Some claim the springs were active as recently as the turn of the century. The locals insist that the springs have not been active in the area for some 400 to 500 years.

It is rumored that the initial owner of Panamint Springs was the niece of William Cody who started the resort as stopping spot on the road to Death Valley in 1937.

Facilities: Gas & propane fuel, mini mart, 14 unit motel and campground with showers, R. V. spots (with & without hookups), a quality restaurant, knowledgeable tourist information, trees, outstanding views of the desert & an unimproved airstrip. Panamint Springs is also available for day use and for conferences.

PANAMINT SPRINGS RESORT
P. O. BOX 395
RIDGECREST, CA. 93556
RESERVATIONS & INFORMATION: (775) 482-7680,
.www.deathvalley.com

DARWIN FALLS
Mile 88 (to turn-off)

A waterfall in the middle of the desert? That's right, in fact if you can find the trail you can see not only one 40-foot waterfall you can climb to view the upper Darwin Fall.

The turnoff to Darwin Falls is located south west of Highway 190 just 1 mile west of Panamint Springs Resort. Some 2 1/4 miles up this dirt road is the signed turn off to the Darwin Falls trailhead that is 1/4 mile up the side road. (Past the Darwin Falls turnoff, it is a four-wheel drive only road. It eventually ends up in Darwin (a ghost town) some 6 miles past the falls turn off.

The hike to the falls is about a mile over an increasingly harder trail that winds back and forth over a stream. There are several boulder climbs and other obstacles. .

Once past the turn off to Darwin Falls the still two lane road becomes fairly steep as it climbs out of Panamint Valley. Soon the roadway is traveling along picturesque Rainbow Canyon. Near the summit there is a scenic pullout with a view that makes the stop worthwhile. At the pullout there is a plaque marking the spot as the Father Crowley Point Monument. (Father Crowley was known as the "padre of the desert," in part for the help he gave those displaced by the appropriation of much of Owens Valley by the City of Los Angeles.)

After traversing a series of rolling hills the road drops to the northeastern shore of Owens Lake on its way into Lone Pine to rejoin Highway 395 at the Interagency Visitors Center.

INTERSECTION OF ROAD TO DARWIN
Mile 98
Elevation 4,740'
No Services

The community of Darwin, no services, is located 6 miles west of the highway. Just west of the town are the remnants of numerous mining operations, including housing, which have been closed for many years. There is a 4-WD road from the east end of Darwin that leads to Darwin Falls, best to check its condition before using.

INTERSECTION HIGHWAYS 190 AND 136
Mile 118

LEFT (HIGHWAY 190)
Turning left the road goes along the southern shore of Owens Lake, past Dirty Socks Hot Springs 15 miles to Highway 395 in Olancha, which is 23 miles south of Lone Pine, the "long way there."

STRAIGHT AHEAD (HIGHWAY 136)
Highway 136 goes along the eastern shore of Owens Lake,. following the base of the Inyo Mountains, directly to Lone Pine, 19 miles.

CERRO GORDO ACCESS ROAD
Mile 121
Cerro Gordo Elevation 8,500'
Food & lodging by prior arraignment

At a height of almost a mile above Owens Lake the 8 mile drive to Cerro Gordo can be quite a test for a vehicle both in going up and to the vehicle's brakes coming back down.

CERRO GORDO SIDE TRIP

GETTING THERE: Signed "Cerro Gordo" dirt road, 1/8th mile east of Keeler. This road is also referred to as the infamous "Yellow Grade Road." The site is some 8 miles up the hill from the highway. Important note: This road is maintained; however it is quite steep and narrow in areas. Your vehicle should be in good operating condition with GOOD BRAKES. Please heed the signs along the road and DO NOT EXPLORE THE MINES! The trip up the mountain is quite interesting even to the amateur geologist. There are area where the strata of the earth has come to the surface and then been driven to a 90 degree angle. The views on the way to Cerro Gordo can be magnificent. Use care, as there can be other traffic on this narrow road

Spanish for "Fat Hill," early exploratory mining was begun here by the Spanish and others prior to the 1860s. In the mid-1860s serious mining began in this mountainous area. Cerro Gordo is located at about 8,500-foot altitude, just about a mile above Owens Lake.

During the late 1860s Los Angeles was in dire financial trouble. The 4,000 inhabitants had become the victims of a drought and other financial misfortunes. Suddenly the mines of Cerro Gordo were shipping tons of silver and lead were now pouring from the deep mines at Cerro Gordo and down through the desert to the Port of Los Angeles. Soon fully one-third of all of the business through the Port of Los Angeles was from Cerro Gordo! The Los Angeles News on February 2, 1872 stated, "To this city Cerro Gordo trade is invaluable. What Los Angeles now is, is mainly due to it. It is the silver cord that binds our present existence. Should it unfortunately severed, we would inevitably collapse."

THE HUGE HOIST HOUSE WHICH OVERLOOKS THE TOWN OF CERRO GORDO

It is somewhat ironic that in 1913 the same City of Los Angeles drained Owens Lake in order to water its lawns and flush its toilets. The same lake that was in part responsible for the transportation of the lead and silver that saved Los Angeles from "inevitable collapse!"

Cerro Gordo was to become one of the largest lead mines in the country in addition to producing tons of silver. The ore was to come from a depth of 1150' and some 37 miles of tunnels on 7 levels. Cerro Gordo grew to a "town" of some 4800 hearty people.

The Cerro Gordo of today is unique. While many people study history, Jody Stewart and Mike Patterson literally lived it. Jody's family has long been involved with Cerro Gordo, even to the point of a relative who lived here during the last century. Judy and Mike set about to restore this historic spot to its earlier condition. All of this work is being done without the aid of grants or other government assistance.

Using volunteers including Scout groups, churches and other groups these two individuals set course to restore the Cerro Gordo of old and open it up to others for learning and sharing.

Activities also include offering underprivileged children an opportunity to share and learn the history found here

The 1904 bunkhouse has been remodeled and now serves as accommodations for up to 14. The 1,200 square foot Belshaw House, built in 1868 features two bedrooms with queen-sized beds. The old general store now contains numerous artifacts from the area.

Cerro Gordo is now available as a "bed & breakfast." The electricity, which was brought here in 1916, is still available and pure water is now pumped from the depths of the mine. The 1871 American Hotel sports an authentic 1870's dining room.

An option to the indoor facilities for the purist history buff who wants to rough it

We are sorry to report that Jody Stewart has passed away. Mike, her husband, is continuing the restoration of Cerro Gordo.

For further information and current road conditions:
CERRO GORDO MINES
P.O. BOX 221
KEELER, CA. 93530
Ph/FAX (760) 876-5030
www.geocities.com/yosemite/1911/cerro2.htm AND http://www.cerrogordo.com

RETURN TO HIGHWAY 136 - END OF SIDE TRIP

KEELER
Mile 122
Elevation at Keeler 3609'
No services.

Keeler was an additional support center for the mining activities in the mountains above it. A 1,200-foot wharf, which had been built of low-grade slag extended into the lake and allowed the minerals from the mines to be loaded aboard steamboats for shipment across Owens Lake on its way to Los Angeles. Transporting across the lake saved days in transporting materials and supplies to and from Los Angeles.

During the 1860s & 1870s Keeler boasted of a population of 7,500 hearty souls. This was the location of hotels, gambling halls and saloons among other services for the miners and mill hands. Today Keeler is a small residential community on the edge of a dried up Owens Lake.

SWANSEA (site):
Mile 126

In 1869 this became the site of The Owens Lake Silver & Lead Furnace. Swansea was once a busy milling and supply center servicing the various mines in the Inyo Mountains above it. The California Historic Landmark tells us that this mill, combined with the output of the mill at Cerro Gordo, was as high as 150 bars of silver every 24 hours, each bar weighing 83 pounds.

For many years the Swansea area was a haven for rock, mineral and archeological collectors. In 1997 floodwaters, the result of El Nino, washed away the historic site.

Today the California Historical Marker and the remnants of a narrow gauge railroad car mark the site. (NOTE there is a TRUE 4-wheel-drive road to Cerro Gordo located just west of the residence in Swansea. This residence is occupied. The condition of this quite lengthy route should be checked prior to attempting it. This is NOT the main road into Cerro Gordo. The main road to Cerro Gordo is located 1/8th mile east of Keeler.)

JUNCTION HIGHWAY 395 & INTERAGENCY VISITOR CENTER
(TWO MILES SOUTH OF LONE PINE)
Mile 137

END OF LOOP TRIP

SIDE TRIP TO CERRO GORDO

Right, east, on Hwy. 190 at the junction of Hwy 395, travels the southern side of Owens Lake.

ATTRACTIONS

Access to ***Dirty Socks Hot Springs**,

Joins loop side trip "B" on Page at Hwy 136. ***Cerro Gordo ghost town & mine, Keeler and Swansea.*** Also gives access to Death Valley National Park, Panamint Valley by going right, south, at Junction of Highways 190 & 136.

(*Indicates SIDE TRIPS from LOOP TRIP)

returns to Hwy 395 (34 miles total), 2 miles south of Lone Pine

NO SERVICES IN ROUTE

DIRTY SOCKS SPRINGS
No Services
Mile 4 1/2

Located via a short all-weather dirt road this hot spring is located at the shore of what was once Owens Lake.

This location affords an excellent view on the Sierra Mountains as well as a look at the old lakebed.

Now it is not clear as to whether or not the spring earned its name from its color, or its odor. While we have, on occasion, seen people bathing in the springs, we have somehow managed to avoid the experience.

Dirty Socks Springs reflect the snow capped Sierras, and the trash barrels.

SIDE TRIP TO ONION VALLEY FROM INDEPENDENCE
13 Miles
Camping, hiking trails, chemical toilets, NO SERVICES
Market Street, becoming Onion Valley Road west of Highway 395 in Independence

Leaving Independence and passing the Mary Austin Home and the Eastern California Museum, the road crosses the rolling foothills located at the base of the Sierra Nevada Mountains before passing the Seven Pines area and Gray's Meadow campgrounds.

This view from the upper portion of the Onion Valley Road shows the Seven Pines and Grey's Meadow camping areas. In the background is the Owens Valley with the Owens riverbed in the background.

The higher the road travels the more it twists and turns giving the traveler a series of dramatic views of not only the valley below but of the mountains ahead. In several spots Independence Creek crosses the road as it charges down the mountain.

Several waterfalls bracket Onion Valley, which is a green oasis surrounded on three sides by rocky peaks of the High Sierra.

In addition to the beauty of the area, one of the first things we noted were a pair of signs; "Elevation 9,200 feet" read the first sign. The second sign was a little more ominous, "WARNING - CITATION ISSUED FOR FOOD LEFT UNPROTECTED FROM BEARS."

While having encountered other bear warning signs and bear-proof food "safes," this was first warning we had seen of a possible citation, which really made sense to us.

In addition to offering spectacular views and beautiful camping areas, complete with fire pit/barbeques picnic tables and clean chemical toilets, Onion Valley is also the trailhead for several trails which extend further into the High Sierras.

One of the more popular trails out of Onion Valley is the Kearsarge Pass Trial which takes the hiker 5 miles to the crest of the Sierra Nevada mountain range. There is also pack station located here.

Water comes cascading down the southern side of Onion Valley rushing towards the campground as it heads down the mountain

The Onion Valley campground is located amongst the Aspens, Pines and other greenery at the base of the rugged tree lined peaks of the crest of the High Sierra Mountains

SECTION TWO
INDEPENDENCE TO BISHOP
60 MILES
With side trips

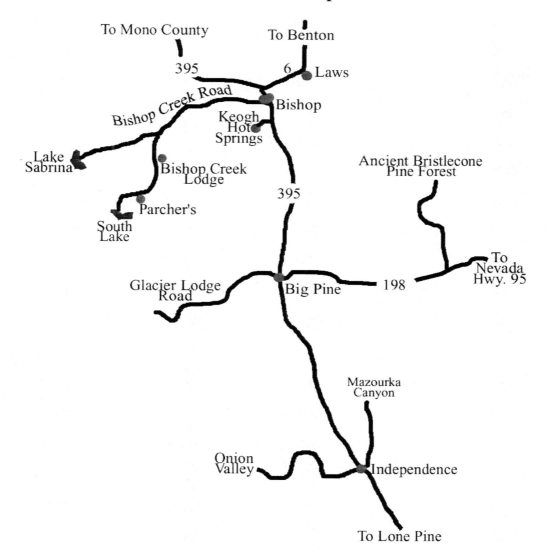

MAP IS NOT TO SCALE

MOUNT WHITNEY FISH HATCHERY
3/4 of a mile north of Independence, Hatchery Road, west side of Highway 395.
Open daily 8 am - 5pm

This is the Mount Whitney Fish Hatchery, not a castle

Located a mile west of the highway, on Hatchery Road, is one of the most unusual buildings to be found anywhere in the area. The main building at the Mount Whitney Fish Hatchery was built by the local citizens in 1916, and donated for use as a hatchery. This facility produces some 15 million rainbow, brown and golden trout eggs annually.

The inside of the hatchery is open for self-guided tours. Additionally, there is a duck pond, filled with giant trout complete with a coin-operated trout food machine, just east of the main building

While there are numerous fish hatcheries in the area, the Mount Whitney hatchery is the most unusual and certainly worth the short trip in order to visit it
.
FORT INDEPENDENCE COMMANDER'S HOUSE - SITE
East side of Highway 395, opposite Mount Whitney Fish Hatchery

Directly across the highway from the fish hatchery, on the east side of Highway 395, is the original location of the Fort Independence commander's house. Originally constructed in 1872 after the home's original adobe buildings were destroyed in the earthquake that year,

The home, which is now located in Independence, on Highway 395 at Main Street is open for inspection at various time of the year. Call the Eastern California Museum (760) 878-0364 for information.

The ruins of the old fort itself are long gone and while Fort Independence did become a factor in the history of the Owens Valley, it is but a memory now

DIVISION CREEK CALTRANS ROADSIDE REST
(Eastern Sierra scenic Byway)
Mile 10

BIG PINE (*Eastern Sierra scenic Byway*)
Mile 27
Gas, food, lodging, supplies
Elevation 3,700'

Big Pine refers to itself as the "Vacation Hub of the Eastern Sierra." Hiking, fishing, camping hot springs and packing are all located within a half-day of Big Pine. The southernmost and largest glaciers in the Sierra Nevada are found in Big Pine Canyon east of Big Pine.

In earlier days the Big Pine area sported a row of handsome Yellow Pines, which ran the length of the creek, from which Big Pine got its name. Eventually all of these beauties were chopped down. Today the tall stately pine tree at the intersection of Highways 395 and 168, planted in honor of President Theodore Roosevelt, is the lone remnant of the once prolific beauties.

Intersection of Hwys 395 & 168 is marked by this pine tree

Big Pine Creek just east of the site of now destroyed Glacier lodge

Gold is still found in areas north and west of Big Pine, maps are available at the chamber office.

To the west of our Highway 395 is Glacier Lodge Highway, giving access into the reaches of the Eastern Sierra. Glacier Lodge Highway reaches an altitude in excess of 7,700 feet at the site of the Glacier Lodge, 11 miles west of Highway 395. While the lodge burnt down in 1998, there cabins available, trailer and camping facilities and day use facilities. This area also offers fishing, Ice & rock climbing (including access Palisade Glacier.) There is a store with supplies at the end of the road. This roadway takes the traveler past numerous campgrounds at it follows along Big Pine Creek. *GLACIER LODGE RESORT,* (760) 938-2837, www.395.comglacierlondge/

Big Pine Chamber of Commerce & Visitor's Center
126 S. Main Street/P.O. Box 23 Big Pine, CA 93513
(760) 938-2114, www.bigpine.com

SIDE TRIPS FOUND ALONG HIGHWAY 168, EAST OF HIGHWAY 395
ANCIENT BRISTLECONE FOREST, 23 MILES.
DEATH VALLEY ACCESS (VIA ONLY PARTIAL UNIMPROVED ROADS.)
NO SERVICES! **NEXT SERVICES ARE AT GOLDFIELD NEVADA, 97 MILES**

This short section of Hwy.168 is only one lane wide!

RV ALERT: While the access all of the way from Highway 395 to the Visitor's Center at Schulman Grove is via paved road, Highway 168 East is steep and has numerous sharp curves and access by RVs, motor homes and trailers is not recommended.

State Highway 168 east of Highway 395 offers numerous destinations to travelers. Additionally, there are group campgrounds located along Highway 168 in the vicinity and along White Mountain Road.

ZURICH STATION (site)
Mile 1.8

Several miles east of Highway 395 on the north side of Highway 168 are the remnants of Zurich Station. Not much here. This was once one of the stations which the "Slim Princess" frequented along narrow gauge railroad line which ran from Mound House, Nevada to Keeler, located on the north shore of now dry Owens Lake, California. (More information on this railroad line is found in the section on the Laws Museum on page 53.

Some of the remnants of Zurich Station just off Highway 168, east of Highway 395

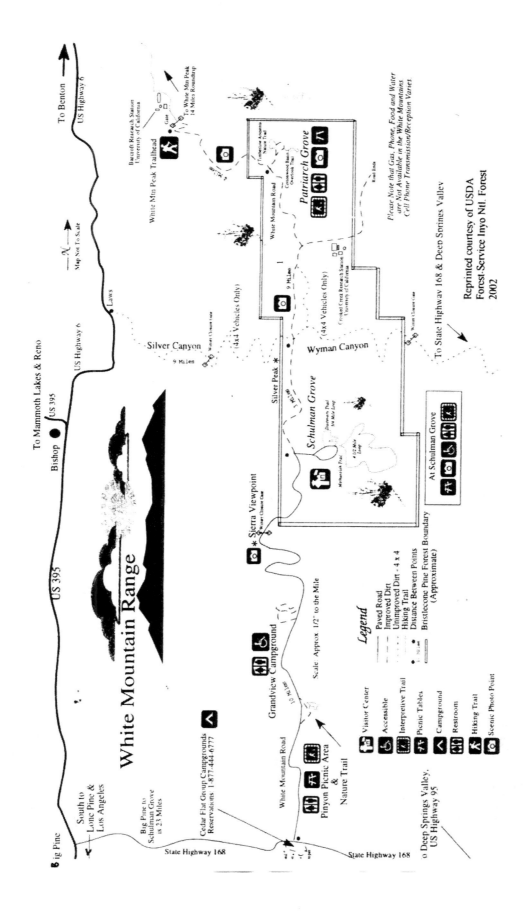

ACCESS TO SALINE VALLEY, EUREKA DUNES & DEATH VALLEY
Mile 2.3 (Right turn Death Valley Road)

Access to *Saline Valley, Eureka Sand Dunes and Northern Death Valley* **RV ALERT:** These access roads are designed for high-clearance and 4WD vehicles. *GETTING THERE:* Highway 168 2.3 miles east of Highway 395, turn right on *Death Valley Road.*

Once the highway leaves the valley it begins to wind its way through the Inyo Mountains. The road contains numerous switchbacks and really tight curves.

ANCIENT BRISTLECONE PINE FOREST
Access Mile 12.9 (left turn, White Mountain Road)
(It is an additional 10 miles from the access road to the forest area.)
(No services, no water.)
(Chemical toilets at the visitor center and at Sierra Point and picnic areas and campgrounds)
FEE AREA
(The fee will be collected at the entrance or at the Schulman Visitor Center)

Located along White Mountain Road, the entrance road, there are designated picnic and camping areas. There is no fee for either other than the entrance fee. The camping and picnic areas offer chemical toilet facilities in addition to fire rings and picnic tables.

SIERRA VIEW VISTA POINT: Mile 21.

From an altitude of over 9,300 feet one may look down from the White Mountains upon the town of Bishop, over 5,000 feet below, and across the Owens Valley to the High Sierra Mountains with peaks in excess of 13,000 feet.

This view from Sierra View Vista Point contains the town of Bishop and some High Sierra Mountains

Access into the Schulman Grove, named for the scientist who determined the age of the pines, is via paved road. While there are other groves, north of the Schulman Grove, all of the other roads in the forest are unpaved but should be easily driven in the family car. Care should be exercised during and following bad weather

The oldest living trees on our planet, some at over 4,700 years old, these rugged trees live on the side of 10,000 to 11,000 feet tall windswept hills. The oldest pine, Methuselah, is unmarked in order to prevent erosion and vandalism.

While the Bristlecone Pines are found in numerous areas throughout the west, the oldest and largest numbers of trees are found here.

The Schulman Grove Visitor Center's scenic location

There is an interpretive center located at the Schulman Grove, which contains exhibits and information for self-guided interpretive trails.

Two of the most popular trails, Methuselah, 4 1/2 mile loop, and Discovery Trail, 3/4-mile loop begin at the visitor center.

Patriarch Grove is located 13 miles beyond Schulman Grove and in addition to spectacular views and numerous Bristlecone Pines, offers spectacular view in route in addition to toilet facilities, picnic tables and outdoor displays.

It is interesting to note that while these trees are quite old, they are not that large. The average growth of a Bristlecone Pine is reported to be $1/100^{th}$ of an inch, or less, annually!

Usually open from mid-May through November 1st, CLOSED IN WINTER. Taking ANY wood out of the forest is strictly prohibited.

Additional pictures of the area will be found in the color picture section of this book.

ADDITIONAL INFORMATION: USDA Forest Service, Inyo National forest, 798 W Main Street, Bishop, CA 93514. Recorded Information: (760) 873-2500.
www.r5.fs.fed.us/inyo/wc/bcp/

ACCESS TO NEVADA HIGHWAY 95
Mile 97 (84 miles east of Ancient Bristle Cone Pine Forest entrance, off of **California Highway 168 which becomes Nevada Highway 266 at the state line.**
NO SERVICES EN ROUTE.

Nearest services 15 miles *north* of the junction of Highway 266 on Nevada Highway 95 at Goldfield, Nevada (a total of 112 miles from Big Pine,) an interesting "ghost town which is still alive. Services also available in Beatty, Nevada, 51 miles south of the Junction of the junction of Nevada Highway 266 (148 miles from Big Pine.) Beatty, Nevada also gives access to the famous ghost town on Rhyolite, to Death Valley (via paved road.) Las Vegas is 170 miles south of Beatty on Highway 95.

Highways 168 and 266 are much not as winding or steep once one leaves the White Mountains, a few miles east of access to the Ancient Bristlecone Forest

END OF SIDE TRIP

CONTINUING NORTH ON HIGHWAY 395

OWENS VALLEY RADIO OBSERVATORY
Mile 30 (seen to the east at this point)
(Access is limited to groups with reservations only)

The huge disks, measuring from two to one hundred and thirty feet in diameter, are listening to and measuring things throughout our galaxy and beyond.

There is a good view of the disks from Highway 168 as it climbs out of the Owens Valley en route to the Ancient Bristlecone Pine Forest.

If you have a group wishing to listen in on ET, call (760) 938-2075 X109 to arrange a group tour.

KEOUGH'S HOT SPRINGS
Mile 33
Access Keough's Hot Springs Road west, 1 mile
Fee Area
Swimming, wading, lodging, camping snack bar

Today's Keough Hot Springs pool

Throughout history, everyone from the Native Americans who once inhabited the area to the affluent from Hollywood to highway travelers have used these hot springs. Six hundred gallons a minute of 127-degree water feed the largest hot springs pool in the Eastern Sierra.

The pool is drained and the walls of the pool area cleaned on a weekly basis.

Opened with the first pool in 1919, remnants of the past remain at the springs. In addition to the old pool building, which was built in 1919, there are several of the original cabins located about the grounds.

Open to the public, Keough's Hot Springs also offers the swimmers and soakers the choice of a 40'x 100' swimming pool or a 24' X 40' wading pool

The original, 1919 Keough Pool facility

Keough's Hot Springs are now owned operated by the Brown Family who operate various other recreational facilities in the eastern Sierra area

Keough's Hot Springs is like an oasis, featuring rolling green lawns and lots of shade trees. There are several trails which lead out from the springs area that appeared to be quite attractive as they led through the foothills surrounding the hot springs.

For reservations and Information: (760) 872-4670, www.keoughshotsprings.com

BISHOP
(*Eastern Sierra scenic Byway*)
Mile 60 (267 miles total)
Elevation 4,140'
Full service city, *Laws Railroad Museum, Piute/Shoshone Cultural Museum,*

On April 6, 1862, 5 ¼ miles southeast of Bishop a battle between newly arrived citizens of Owens River Valley and Paiute and Shoshone Indians took place. While little is known of the battle there is a monument to it located at Bishop Creek Battleground, 50 yards southeast of the intersection of Highway 168 and Bishop Creek Road.

The current history of Bishop begins August 22, 1861 when Samuel Bishop, his wife and some drovers arrived in the area of what is today Bishop. Along with this party came 500 to 600 head of cattle and some 50 horses. Also, herds of sheep were soon being grazed across the northern portion of the valley.

It was soon determined that the northern end of Owens Valley was user friendly to a variety of crops in addition to the livestock which was initially brought into the area. Today such diverse crops as potatoes, alfalfa, wheat, corn and celery are grown here. Soon orchards were producing figs, apples, walnuts, peaches, pears, plums, berries and grapes as a result of the climate and soil found in the Bishop area.

In 1883 the narrow gauge Carson & Colorado Railroad came to Bishop and with the railroad the trade in this growing town increased. The "Slim Princess" narrow gauge engine, now located in the Law's Museum north of Bishop, played a major part in the growth of Bishop.

In 1937 Erick Schat's Bakery, on Main Street began baking "Sheepherder's Bread" and has been baking it ever since.

Today Bishop is well known to numerous types of vacationers. The proximity to the eastern Sierra with its multitude of winter and summer activities has made this city a hub for many "out of towners."

Recently Bishop was named "America's Coolest Mountain Town." With its proximity to the High Sierras and the abundance of both summer and winter outdoor activities this tree filled high –desert community rivals many alpine settings.

A wide variety of eateries are to be found in Bishop.

Every Memorial Day Weekend, for as long as anyone can recall, the town has become filled with mules for Bishop's annual "Mule Days." Labor Day Weekend brings the annual rodeo to town where the locals compete with the professionals. *Mule Days Information (888) 395-3952*

The Bishop Mural Society has been responsible for numerous historically oriented murals place on key buildings in town. More information on these murals can be obtained through *The Lady*

Early morning along the western shore of Mono Lake (Page 69)

The schoolhouse in Bodie still contains the desks. Its almost as if the students were on vacation (Page 77)

Early morning at the beaver ponds located a mile above Lundy Lake. (Page 72)

Bishop Creek as it passes through Parcher's Resort. The trout can almost be seen in the stream (Page 51)

Water rushing over the rocks at the northern end of Onion Valley (Page 38)

The high altitude Ancient Bristlecone forest is a place of rugged beauty (Page 44)

The Old House in Benton Hot Springs features many historic items, inside and out! (Page 92)

The historic narrow gauge "Slim Princess" in retirement at the Law's museum (Page 53)

The Hot Creek Geothermal site is just that as steam rises from the usually cold creek (Page 60)

Mount Morrison towers over Aspen lined Convict Lake in the fall (Page 59)

Bug Art Gallery, 462 Rose Street, Bishop CA 93514. (760) 873-3600 FAX (760) 872-2816
www.thesierraweb.com/bishopmuralmoreinfo.html

Today there are four reservations within the Owens Valley which are the homes for many of the Paiute and Shoshone who live within the valley.

> BISHOP AREA Chamber of Commerce & Visitors Bureau
> 690 N. Main Street
> Bishop, CA. 93514
> (760) 873-8405 www.bishopvisitor.com

Also located in Bishop is the Bureau of Land Management, office that is responsible for managing thousands of acres of public land in the area surrounding Bishop.

> *Bureau of Land Management*
> Bishop Field Office
> 785 N. Main St. Ste E
> Bishop, CA 93514
> (760) 872-4881 www.ca.blm.gov/bishop/index.html

SIDE TRIP
BISHOP CREEK CANYON AND LAKE SABRINA RECREATION AREAS

HIGHWAY 168 WEST/WEST LINE STREET (South end of Bishop)
SOUTH LAKE, BISHOP CREEK CANYON, 19 MILES
Fishing, lodging, fishing, food, fishing, hiking, fishing, supplies, camping
LAKE SABRINA, CARDINAL RESORT AREA 16 MILE
Fishing, lodging, fishing, food, fishing, hiking, fishing, supplies, camping
Paved roads

The Paiute Shoshone Indian Culture Center, West Line Street

Turn west onto West Line Street from Highway 395 for one of the more interesting and diverse areas of Bishop. One mile west of Highway 395, at 2200 West Line Street, on the north side of the highway is the Owens Valley Paiute Shoshone Indian Culture Center and Museum which is open to the public and contains, among other things a complete look at the local Native American cultures and their evolution throughout the years. The center is open 10 a.m. to 4 p.m. most of the time.

Bishop Creek as it passes through Parcher's

Continuing westward at a point 3 1/2 miles west of Highway 395 is California Historic Marker #208 which marks the location of the San Francis Ranch, the first ranch in the area. In 1861 Samuel A. Bishop and his wife settled in the area and began ranching.

At mile 5 1/4 is California Historic Marker # 811 which marks the approximate location of battle which took place in the vicinity between the white settlers and the Paiute and Shoshone inhabitants of the area. The details of the battle have been lost in obscurity, however there are still isolated reports of "scalping" within the Indian gambling Casino at the north end of Bishop. These reports are generally from spouses of the "victims."

Just past this point our highway begins a rather steep climb through a scenic canyon from Bishop with an elevation of 4,100 feet to our destinations with altitudes in the neighborhoods in the 8,500 to 9,800-foot range

While the Lake Sabrina Road is a fairly steep one, there are not excessive curves en route to Sabrina Lake. South Bishop Lake Road contains quite a few sharp curves past Bishop Creek Lodge en route to and Bishop creek Lodge, Parcher's Resort and South Lake.

BISHOP CREEK RECREATIONAL AREA & SOUTH LAKE

At mile 11.7 north of Highway 395, is the turn-off (Left, or south) for South Lake Road. This road follows the scenic Bishop Creek and the more placid Green Creek 7 miles to South Lake.

At mile 16.7, 5 miles from the turn-off from Highway 168 is the *Bishop Creek Lodge*. Built in 1928 the rustic lodge offers food, cabins, supplies and a saloon. The restaurant is open for continental breakfasts, lunch and dinner. The store offers provisions and a large tackle selection. The cabins are full housekeeping and offer barbeques and picnic tables.

Bishop Creek Lodge

Bishop Creek Lodge, like many of the other resorts in the area, offers that old-fashioned hospitality which includes insights into the best fishing spots.

Bishop Creek Lodge
2100 S. Bishop Creek Road
Bishop, CA 93514
(760) 873-4484
bishopcreekresorts,com

The road past Bishop Creek Lodge is not plowed during the winter and is closed by snow.

About a mile past Bishop Creek Lodge is the *Twin Lakes* fishing area.

Parcher's Resort and Rainbow Pack Station is located 6 miles south of Highway 168 at mile 21 from Highway 395. Located at an altitude of 9,260 feet this rustic resort is bracketed by Bishop Creek and Green creek between the tree lined Coyote Ridge and Table Mountain.

The John Muir Wilderness is right out the back door offering a full variety of trails leading to lakes, meadows and streams. Additionally there is a selection of old mining roads and lots of rocks to climb in the area.

Cabin #1 at Parcher's Resort, sitting beside Bishop Creek

Many of the rustic cabins here are on the banks of either of the two streams which surround the resort. The cabins all include bathroom facilities and some of them offer kitchens. There are also RV facilities with full hookups available in the camp. There are fish cleaning facilities located at the store.

The combination store, coffee shop and office is open from 8 to 8. A continental breakfast-complimentary for lodge guest-is served from 8 - 10 a.m. with sandwiches and deserts served after that time.

Alternating Saturday nights are Barbeque night at Parcher's Resort. We have found Parcher's Resort to be one of the most enjoyable, scenic and hospitable places we have visited in our travels.

Located just a mile from South Lake, boat rentals are available.

At the foot of the Dam for South Lake there is a weir pond, in which a lot of fishermen in waders can often be seen.

South Lake is located one mile past Parcher's at the end of the paved road. There is a launch ramp, boat rental and shore fishing here at the base of the towering Sierras. There are several trailheads here which lead into the smaller lakes, streams and other scenic locations in the area.

Parcher's Resort
2100 South Lake Road
Bishop, CA 93514
(760) 873 4177
e-mail: bspcrk@schat.com

**END OF SIDE TRIP DOWN SOUTH LAKE ROAD
RETURN TO LAKE SABRINA ROAD, HIGHWAY 168 WEST**

Turning left, back onto Highway 168, will put us just 4 miles from Lake Sabrina as we continue to climb towards Lake Sabrina,

Approximately 1 1/2 miles south of the Bishop Creek Road Intersection is the community of Aspendell. The multitude of Aspen trees which follow the creek through this community make the name of the area an obvious one.

Turning into Aspendell and then following the signs northward along the creek-side road for a short distance takes us to the *Cardinal Village Resort*.

The *Cardinal Village Resort* started life as a mine in 1885. In fact some of the guest cabins in use today at the resort started life as cabins housing the workers and families. The original foundation and the woodenhead of the mine are but a short walk from the resort.

This resort offers fishing, store, cafe, hiking, fish cleaning facilities and even gold panning. Open all year ice skating, cross-country skiing and snowshoeing are available.

Cardinal Resort
(760) 873-4789 www.caardinalvillageresort.com
Route 1 Box A3, Bishop, CA 93514

Lake Sabrina is 1 1/2 miles south of Cardinal Resort and offers fishing, boating and camping.

END OF SIDE TRIP, BISHOP CREEK CANYON & SABRINA AREAS
LAWS RAILROAD MUSEUM AND HISTORICAL SITE

Map courtesy of Laws Museum

Laws' Railroad Museum (California Historic Landmark #953) is located 4 ½ miles northeast of Bishop off of Highway 6. Not only is Laws Railroad Museum a state landmark it is also listed on the National Registry of Historical Places, Department of the Interior. The museum is operated by the Bishop Museum and Historical Society, www.visitbishop.com.

For the train or the history buff, the 11 acres at Laws offers the enthusiast an interesting place to visit. Laws Railroad Museum contains not only a complete narrow-gauge train, the "Slim Princess," but also includes a completely furnished historic town.

Outside are found displays of mining equipment, farm equipment in addition to the original 1883 Laws depot The displays even include the original 1883 roundtable.

The historic buildings located at Laws Railroad Museum contain a variety of historic exhibits.

From August of 1883 through April 30, 1960 train service ran through this location. The initial train service was to Keeler, located on the eastern shore of Owens Lake.

It was the combination of the closing of the local mines and the cost of trucking becoming cheaper than the railroad that ended railroading through Laws.

While many of the buildings located at Laws were moved here to save them from destruction, some of them have been standing here for over 100 years.

The combination indoor museum and gift shop offers not only a look at history but also the opportunity take some of it home.

Laws is open all year from 10 am to 4 pm. Take Highway 6 four and one half miles north of Bishop. At the 90 degree LEFT in the highway turn right on Silver Canyon Road. The museum is just a few feet east of Highway 6.

Information: (760) 873-5950, www.sierraweb.com

BISHOP AREA Chamber of Commerce & Visitors Bureau
690 N. Main Street
Bishop, CA. 93514
(760) 873-8405 www.bishopvisitor.com
RESET ODOMETER TO ZERO AT BISHOP (GOOD PLACE TO GAS UP)

There is an Indian gambling casino located on the north side of Bishop--probably so that people can leave their money there, rather than in Nevada.

After leaving the outskirts of Bishop, Highway 395 becomes divided as it begins its ascent into the higher portion of the eastern Sierra Nevada.

Whitney Portal Store at the foot of Mount Whitney, page 15

MONO COUNTY
(SHERWIN GRADE TO THE NEVADA STATE LINE)

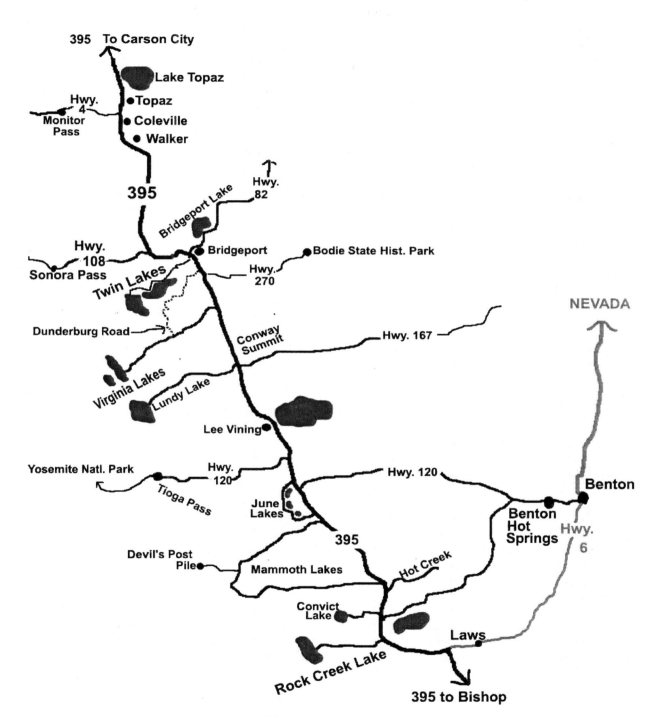

MAP IS NOT TO SCALE

SECTION THREE
MONO COUNTY (SHERWIN GRADE TO THE NEVADA STATE LINE)
120 MILES

SIDE TRIP "D"
Mammoth Lakes area & Devils Postpile National Monument
This side trip is described in detail on Page 58.
ATTRACTIONS:
Mammoth Lakes & *Old Mammoth, *Devils Postpile National Monument, *numerous lakes

SIDE/ LOOP TRIP "E"
Virginia Lakes Road to Dunderburg Rd to Highway 395
This trip is described in detail on Page 75
ATTRACTIONS:
Green Creek, Green Lake, Dynamo Pond

SIDE TRIP "E"
Highway 120, east, to Highway 6, south, to Bishop
This side trip is described in detail on Page 90
ATTRACTIONS
Southern Mono Lake, Benton Hot Springs, Benton, Bishop

* * * * * *

RESUMING OUR TRIP ON HIGHWAY 395

SHERWIN GRADE SCENIC PULL-OUT
(*Eastern Sierra scenic Byway)*
Mile 18

This particular pullout is on the right side of the divided highway and affords and excellent view of the Sierra Nevada Mountains without having to cross the highway.

SHERWIN SUMMIT
Mile 21
Elevation 7,000'

Our highway remains divided from this point <u>most</u> of the way to Deadman's Summit, 33 miles ahead.

CROWLEY LAKE DRIVE, TOM'S PLACE & LITTLE LAKES VALLEY ACCESS
Mile 23
Elevation 7,080

EAST OF HIGHWAY 395

CROWLEY LAKE: Located in the "open" Long Valley, this large lake is named for Father Crowley, who helped the residents of Owens Valley cope with the loss of their water resources.

This reservoir was formed in 1941 by the city of Los Angeles, and is the largest reservoir in the Owens Valley water system. This man made lake has become a popular fishing location. On opening day of trout season as many as 30,000 fishermen can be found at the lake. No swimming is allowed, as this is a reservoir. In addition to Lake Crowley, the local streams also offer excellent fishing.

The lake is open seasonally and in addition to fishing and camping offers boating, including boat rentals. Information on boat rentals and storage may be obtained from Lake Crowley Fish Camp, P.O. BOX 179 June Lake, CA 93529, (760) 935-4301, http://crowleylakefishcamp.com.

The Crowley Lake General Store features a mini-mart, deli, and a true general store complete with fishing licenses & fishing stories. The store is located 1/2 mile south of Highway 395 on South Landing Road, (760) 935-466, www.fishcrowlylake.com.

This road gives access to the dam and the southern portion of the lake. The other access point to Crowley Lake is at Hilton Creek, 3 3/4 miles north on Highway 395.

WEST OF HIGHWAY 395, ROCK CREEK ROAD

Tom's Place Resort is a hub of many activities

TOM'S PLACE: Located at the junction of 395 and Rock Creek Road, Tom's Place has been in existence since 1917. Complete with café, bar, store and a lodge this is a popular stopping place and information center for locals and travelers alike. (760) 935-4239. www.tomsplaceresort.com HCR 79 Box 22-A Crowley Lake, CA 93546

ROCK CREEK ROAD: This 12 mile long paved Road follows Rock Creek past Rock Creek Lake, 8 1/2 miles, and into the Little Lakes Valley. There are numerous campgrounds found along the road. Trout fishing, hiking, skiing, mountain biking and mountain climbing are all found in this area, making it one of the more popular areas in the eastern sierra.

ROCK CREEK RESORT is open from late-June through Labor Day Rock Creek Resort, P.O. Box 727, Bishop, CA 93515, www.rockcreeklake.com/resort (760) 935-4311.

ROCK CREEK LODGE is open year-round and offers both winter and summer activities Information: Rock Creek Lodge, HCR 79 BOX 12, Mammoth Lakes, CA 93546, (877) 935-4170. www.rockcreeklodge.com.

Rock Creek Lake is surrounded by 13,000' peaks

CROWLEY LAKE ACCESS
(*Eastern Sierra scenic Byway*)
East
Mile 27.5

Access to the western portion of Crowley Lake to the east and access to Crowley Lake Drive, the BLM campground and the Father Crowley Memorial to the west.

CROWLEY LAKE VISTA POINT
East
Mile 28

A good view of the lake and of much of Long Valley in which it is located can be found here.

MC GEE CREEK ROAD
West
Mile 30,5
Lodging

Access to Mc Gee Creek and to the Mc. Gee Creek Pack Station, 3 1/2 miles.

CROWLEY LAKE DRIVE (North end)
West
Mile 32

Crowley Lake Drive goes south to Tom's Place, parallel with Highway 395.

BENTON CROSSING ROAD
East
Mile 34

Access to Whitmore Pool (Formerly Whitmore Hot Springs,) 1 mile, Benton Crossing (Owens River Access, fishing, camping, store @ Brown's Owens River Campground, (760) 920-0975, 44 miles, junction Highway 6, via Highway 120 East from Lee Vining, at Benton (Benton/Benton Hot Springs are described on page 92) 46 miles, Tonopah, Nevada 126 miles.

A loop trip from this point Highway through Benton Hot Springs, Benton and then south on Highway 6 to re-join Highway 395 in Bishop, just south of the railroad museum in Laws offers scenic views of the White Mountains as the highway travels along their base.

NOTE: Whitmore Pool is not always open.

CONVICT LAKE
West 2 miles paved road
Mile 35

Fishing, boating (rentals available,) picnic tables, camping, horse & bike rentals, lodging, general store, dinner house

Convict Lake was so named (actually renamed) as the result of a prison break in 1871 when twenty-nine prisoners escaped from the Nevada Territorial prison in Carson City.

Six of the train and stage robbers and murderers had headed south towards Owens Valley. Near the town of Aurora the desperados murdered a mail carrier. Immediately the townspeople of Aurora organized a posse and set out after the scoundrels.

The desperados were sited on the shores of what was then referred to as Monte Diablo Lake. Two of the posse were killed in the gun battle that broke out. One of the posse members was Robert Morrison, for whom Mount Morrison (elevation 12,268') on the lake's south shore was named.

All of the fugitives escaped that battle. Eventually all of the escapees, except for one, were caught and either hanged or returned to prison.

A motion picture released in the 1950's "Secret of Convict Lake," mostly filmed in a sound stage, bears no resemblance to the actual story from which the lake got its name.

This beautiful little lake, about a half-mile wide and a mile long, is surrounded on three sides by towering peaks and lined with aspen and other trees, and filled regularly with fish.

Picnic tables are found scattered around the lake and the shore fishing is reported to be good.

Convict Lake Resort: There are rental cabins set among the trees just below the lake with larger cabins for groups also available. The general store is well supplied.

The restaurant at Convict Lake has quite a reputation for its menu and fine dinners. Lunch is served outside under the Aspen trees during July and August.

Information: Convict Lake Resort, Rt1 Box 204, Mammoth Lakes, CA 93546, (760) 934-3800. www.convictlake.com/contact.html (800) 992-2260.

Camping at Convict Lake: Mammoth Ranger Station (760) 924-5500, NO RESERVATIONS: (877) 444-6777, www.fs.fed.us/r5/inyo.

SHERWIN CREEK ROAD ACCESS TO: HOT CREEK ATTRACTIONS, OWENS RIVER ROAD, MAMMOTH/JUNE LAKE AIRPORT

East
Mile 35
Airport access, Hot Creek fish Hatchery 1 mile, Hot Creek Fish Ranch 2 miles, Hot Creek Geological site, 3 ½ miles.

HOT CREEK FISH HATCHERY: Located just east of Highway 395 this hatchery produces 20,000,000 trout eggs per year. Annually 4,000,000 fingerlings and 800,000 catchable sized trout are released from this hatchery annually. The hatchery is open daily, the fish eat daily and someone must feed them, from 8 am to 4:30 pm. (760) 934-2664.

HOT CREEK FLY FISHING RANCH: This unique fishing ranch offers the dry-fly angler an opportunity to catch the big ones, over and over again. The fishing along Hot Creek through this entire area is limited to barbless hooks and it is strictly "catch and release." Lodging and meals along with fishing guides are available. Hot Creek Ranch, Rural Route 1, Box 206, Mammoth Lakes, CA 93546, (888) 695-0774, www.hotcreekranch.com

Located on the bank of Hot Creek, the Hot Creek Fly Fishing Camp offers unusual fishing.

HOT CREEK GEOTHERMAL SITE: As Hot Creek wanders through the area it is periodically heated from below often bringing the temperature to 200 degrees. The parking area has a path leading down into the gorge containing hot springs. There are vault toilets in the parking area. Due to the possibilities of encountering scalding sections of water in the springs and possible reaction to chemicals in the water (a high concentration of arsenic is found in these waters,) swimming is not recommended here. The area is closed from sunset to sunrise.

JUNCTION HIGHWAY 203
SIDE TRIP
(*Eastern Sierra scenic Byway*)
MAMMOTH LAKES & DEVILS POST PILE ACCESS
Mile 37
Right exit (underpass)
Full services, full summer and winter recreational services

Highway 203 exit from Highway 395 to *Mammoth Lakes*, 203 continues west to *Devils Postpile* **(See note on travel restrictions to Devil's Postpile)** Return to Highway 395 either to on Highway 203 east or on the *Mammoth Scenic Loop*, north to a return point on Highway 395 five miles north of the Highway 203 exit starting point.

MAMMOTH LAKES
Elevation 7860"
ATTRACTIONS:
Towns of Mammoth Lakes & Old Mammoth, numerous lakes
Full services, skiing and other winter sports, hot springs, fishing (lakes, river & streams,) hiking, camping, pack stations

Boasting a year-round population of approximately 6,500 people this popular resort area swells in summer and winter by hundreds of recreation minded vacationers. Summer sees the campers, hikers and fishermen. Winter brings the skiers and snowboarders to the famous lift and cross country runs located in the Mammoth area.

Like so many of the communities on the eastern side of the Sierra Mountains, Mammoth began life in the 1800's as a result of miners from the western side of the Sierra Nevadas seeking precious metals for the "other side" of the mountains.

Mining activity began in the Lake Mary area in 1877. Within the nest two years some twenty five hundred souls had come to the Mammoth area. In 1880 the Mammoth Mining Company closed and most of the hearty souls left the area.

Early in the twentieth century a different group of visitors began the arduous journey across the deserts and up the mountain roads into the Mammoth area. Many of these travelers were making the two-day drive from the Los Angeles area to find solitude and recreation in this beautiful area.

When Highway 395 was completed in 1937 the Mammoth area became a many a summer sportsman's destination.

In the 1930's the first ski lift was built in the Mammoth area at McGee Mountain. By 1941 many skiers were making the Mammoth area their destination.

The area was later to became the diversified recreational and cosmopolitan area which it is today. In 1955, the boom that was to become the Mammoth of today began with the first ski run on Mammoth Mountain.

Mammoth Lakes Area

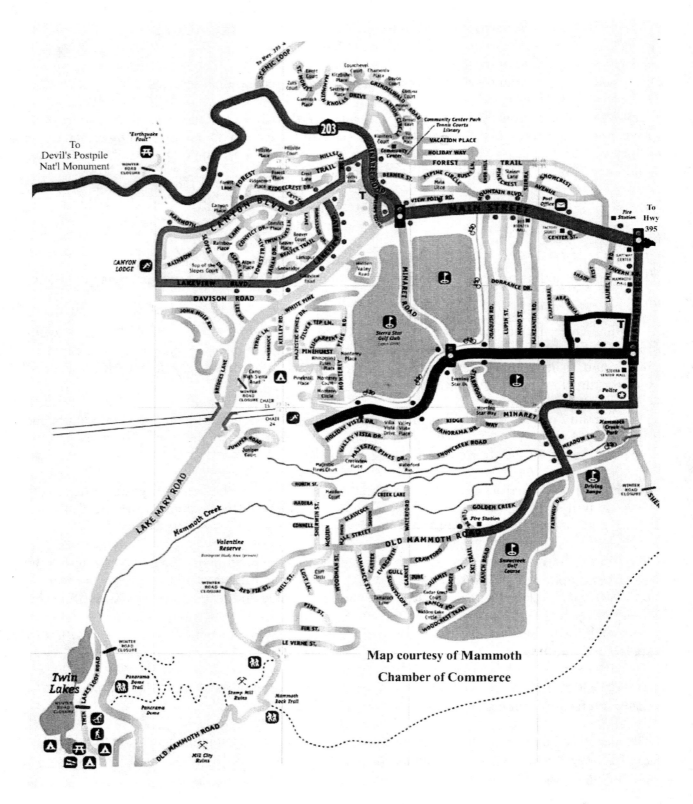

Map courtesy of Mammoth Chamber of Commerce

MAMMOTH MUSEUM: This authentic log cabin was created by a Mammoth pioneer in 1927 and contains numerous of exhibits which give an insight into the history of the area. Everything from mining equipment to memorabilia to photos are found in this rustic cabin located at the edge of scenic meadow.

Open 11am to 6pm from July 1 – Oct 1 mining demonstrations are available weekends. Located south on Sherwin Creek Road, turn south on Old Mountain Road from Highway 203 turn left one mile after crossing the bridge over the creek. Information: (760) 934-6918, (760) 934-8934.

YARTS SHUTTLE BUS SERVICE: Offers bus service from Mammoth to other areas including Yosemite National Park (during the time that the Tioga Pass Road is open,) reservations required. (800) MAMMOTH

ADVENTURE CENTER: Located in the main lodge at Mammoth Mountain the center offers information, bike rentals and repairs, tickets for YARTS shuttle and the scenic bike park in addition to clothing and gear. The center is open summers through September 29th. (760) 934-0706.

LITTLE EAGLE: Located at Juniper Springs offers access to the chairlift ride in addition to complete bike service including rentals, repairs and bike park access. Restaurant, summer concerts, and sportswear are also available here. You may even challenge your friends on the sand volleyball court. (760) 934-0725.

GONDOLA RIDE – CHAIRLIFT RIDES (SUMMER): Panoramic views are available from the 11,053 summit of Mammoth Mountain. The gondola ride is at the Adventure Center and the chairlift is located at Eagle Express at Little Eagle/Juniper Springs. Gondola tickets are available at the Adventure Center and lift tickets are found inside Little Eagle. These lifts are an excellent way to access the upper bike trails in addition to offering immense vista. Open 8am – 5:30pm.

MAMMOTH LAKES VISITORS BUREAU AND CENTRAL RESERVATIONS: P.O. Box 48, Mammoth Lakes CA, 93546. (888) 466-2666. www.VisitMammoth.com. WEATHER AND ROAD CONDITIONS (800) 427-7623

DEVIL'S POSTPILE NATIONAL MONUMENT
Hiking, sightseeing, camping, trout fishing, swimming
(Closed in winter)

Located 13 miles west of downtown Mammoth along Highway 203 is one of the most unusual displays of nature, surrounded by natural beauty to be found anywhere.

Summer travel by private vehicle to Devil's Postpile National Monument is restricted. Shuttle bus service is provided from the Main Lodge at Mammoth Mountain ski area to the monument from 7:30 a.m. to 5:30 p.m. during the summer months. There is a fee for this transportation. Campers at the six campgrounds located in the monument area must obtain permits to drive to and from the campgrounds during the above hours. (Individual camping in the monument area is on a first-come, first-served basis. Group campsites may be reserved through www.reserveusa.com or by calling (877) 444-6777.)

It is an easy 15 minute walk along the San Joaquin River from the parking area to the 60 foot tall Postpile.

Devil's Postpile is rated as the world's finest example of columnar-jointed basalt. These four to seven sided column were formed as lava shrank as it filled the valley. These massive columns are only a portion of nature's exhibits that awaits the visitor to this scenic area.

Located along the routes of both the John Muir and Pacific Crest Trails, the visitor will find meadows and a red-fir forests as they travel south along the San Joaquin River to 100+ high Rainbow falls.

Devil's Postpile National Monument (Photo courtesy NPS)

The Ranger station offers numerous displays, books and maps in addition to campfire programs, guided walks and wilderness permits.

Additional Information: www.nps.gov/depo/pphtml/html or Devil's Postpile Ranger Station
(760) 934-2289 (summer only)

*****

CONTINUING NORTH ON HIGHWAY 395 FROM HIGHWAY 203 EXIT

At about mile 44 our highway begins to climb into the trees. Still divided we will be flanked by trees much of the way north from this point.

NORTH END OF MAMMOTH LAKES SCENIC DRIVE JUNCTION
Mile 42

CRESTVIEW CALTRANS REST AREA <u>WEST</u> SIDE OF HIGHWAY
(*Eastern Sierra scenic Byway*)
Mile 44

NORTHERN END OF OWENS RIVER ROAD JUNCTION
(National Forest Highway #2507, gravel last 11 miles to Hot Springs Road)
Mile 44.5
East

Paved road access to Owens River Ranch, 3 1/2 miles, gravel road through Long Valley, access to Benton Crossing.

DEADMAN'S SUMMIT
Altitude 8,041 feet
Mile 47
JUNCTION GLASS FLOW RD. (West)/ LOGGING CAMP ROAD (East)
Mile 48

These dirt/gravel roads give access to *Obsidian Dome (*Altitude 8611 feet*)* west and to *Bald Mountain Road Lookout* to the right.

SOUTH END OF JUNE LAKE LOOP, JUNCTION HIGHWAY 158 WEST
(*Eastern Sierra scenic Byway)*
Mile 51.4
Full services, skiing and other winter sports, fishing (lakes) hiking, climbing and camping

The June Lake Loop is a 14-mile all-weather road which circles back to Highway 395 after passing 4 major lakes.

These 4 lakes; June Lake, Silver Lake, Gull Lake and Grant Lake have an excellent reputation for large trout.

In addition to providing the summer outdoorsman, or outdoorswoman, with ample activities, the June Lake area offers virtually all of the winter sports one could desire. June Mountain features a ski lift. Additionally, there are numerous opportunities for such activities as snowboarding, ski mountaineering and climbing frozen waterfalls.

June Lake is the first lake awaiting the "Loop" traveler

June Lake Village is 3 miles west of Highway 395 on SR 158. There are numerous motels, hotels and campgrounds found along the loop in addition to other full services.

The northern end of the June Lake Loop is located just NORTH of the junction of Highway 395 & 120

June Lake Chamber of Commerce
P.O. Box 2
June Lake, CA 93529
(760) 548-7584, www.junelakechamber.com

JUNCTION HIGHWAY 120 EAST
ACCESS TO THE SOUTHERN PORTION OF MONO BASIN INCLUDING PANUM CRATER AND SOUTH MONO LAKE AREA, (South Tufa & Navy Beach.)
LOOP TRIP TO BENTON HOT SPRINGS & BENTON VIA HIGHWAY 120 (46 Miles.) AND BISHOP VIA HIGHWAY 6 (DESCRIBED ON PAGE 90). 127 Miles to TONOPAH,

Mile 56.4
No services

PANUM CRATER AND THE MONO CRATERS are located 3 miles east of Highway 395 off of Highway 120 East. Panum Crater is the northernmost of the craters and is located north of Highway 120 via a short road. Access to the Mono Craters South of Highway 120 is limited.

This photo of the Panum Crater and lava dome is Courtesy of the U.S. Geological Survey Volcano Hazards Program

While the Mono craters range in age from 600 to 40,000 years, the Panum crater is not only the youngest and easiest one to access it is probably the most unusual. The Panum crater was created by what is known as a rhyolitic eruption. This crater contains an outer ring and an inner plug dome. Both of these features are accessible by trail and offer a view of the Sierra Nevada Mountains and of the Mono Basin.

The twenty-one volcanic cones, which comprise the Mono Craters, form the youngest mountain range in North America.

SOUTH TUFA is located east of Panum Crater and is one of the more popular spots located around Mono Lake. South Tufa offers the visitor a close-up view of one of the largest tufa groves on the lake. A self guided tour take the visitor among the tours.

South Tufa is a fee area. During the summer naturalist guided tours are available, www.monolake.org.
There are no services, or water, at either South Tufa or Navy Beach. It is advisable to always carry water and some from of sun protection in the Mono Basin during summer.

This picture taken in the late 1980's shows the lower level of Mono Lake, Photo courtesy of Judy Shockly

This early morning fall picture of Mono Lake's wheelchair accessible trail shows frost still on the boards

NAVY BEACH is located just east of South Tufa and a path does connect the two. Since Navy Beach is the most popular launching spot for canoes and kayaks, in addition to being a popular swimming beach, the parking there is limited.

The Tufa Towers at South Beach are slowly being covered by Mono Lake as it deepens

During the summer months the Mono Lake Committee guides canoe tours from Navy Beach. Also, Caldera Kayaks leads kayak tours from here. Contact the Lee Vining Chamber of Commerce, (760) 647-6629 www.leevining.com for details

JUNCTION HIGHWAY 158 WEST, NORTH END OF JUNE LAKE LOOP
Mile 57

JUNCTION HIGHWAY 120 WEST, TIOGA PASS
West (Southern end of the town of Lee Vining)
Mile 61

Tioga Pass Road climbs from Lee Vining at an altitude of 6,780' thirteen miles to Tioga Summit at an elevation of 9.941'. The entrance to Yosemite National Park, a fee area, is adjacent to Tioga summit.

Tioga Pass is closed after the 1st heavy snow

This roadway closes at the first snow of winter and reopens in May or when the road can be kept cleared of snow.

Tioga Pass is the eastern access road into Yosemite National Park. Tuolumne Meadows is 21 miles from Highway 395 and Yosemite Valley is 77 miles. Both Tuolumne Meadows and Yosemite Valley offer gas, food and lodging.

This is a very steep road and being located at a high altitude travel can be quite slow, even in a modern automobile let alone a large vehicle such as a bus, RV or a truck.

The views from this roadway can be spectacular and in many places are uninhibited by guardrails!

LEE VINING, THE MONO BASIN GATEWAY
Mile 61.5
Elevation 6,780'
Full Services, *Mono Lake Committee Information Center & Book Store, Mono Basin Historical Society Museum*

Named for Leland Vining, a prospector, this small town sits on a hillside overlooking Mono Lake.

Lee Vining is the gateway to the Mono Basin, the most famous feature of which is Mono Lake. Lee Vining is known as the place where lands of fire and ice collide with a dramatic collection of geological features.

With its proximity to Mono Lake, the Mono Basin, Tioga Pass and its highway location, this small town can become a beehive of activity for the traveler. While many of the businesses are closed for the winter, all of the many types of services required by a traveler are available year round.

With views of Mono Lake to the northeast, the White Mountains to the east and living in the shadow of the Sierra Nevada Mountains, Lee Vining is an attractive stopping place.

Mono Lake Committee Information Center and Book Store is located at 3rd Street and Highway 395, right in the center of Lee Vining. Open daily from 9 am to 5 pm (stays open later in summer months) and houses information, books, maps and photographs regarding not just Mono Lake but on the entire Mono Basin and general area.

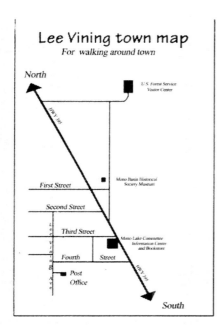

Map courtesy of Mono Lake Newsletter

This is probably one of the most complete information centers on any subject to be found along our highway. Included in the store are photographs and examples of Native American art, much of which is available for sale. (760) 647-6595, www.monolake.org.

The center/bookshop also is the location of the Lee Vining Chamber of Commerce (760) 647-6629www.leevining.com

Mono Basin Historical Society Museum is located on West Main Street (found between 2nd & 3rd Street west of Highway 395.) Open only during the summer. P.O. BOX 31, Lee Vining, CA 93541, (760) 647-6461.

Located to the east, accessible via Highway 120, three miles east of Highway 395, is the Panum Crater, the youngest crater in the youngest mountain range in North America.

At 670 years of age, the youngest Mono crater is a mere baby compared to the mountains surrounding it.

Even the islands located on Mono Lake are volcanoes. The U.S. Geological Survey monitors the region for signs of earthquakes, hot springs and steam vents, which can indicate future volcanic activity. There has been volcanic activity in the basin as recently as 270 years ago.

Black Point, located just off of the north shore of Mono Lake, is an interesting example of volcanic activity. When Black Point erupted 12,000 to 13,000 years ago it was located under Mono Lake. What are left today are fissures, including one which is 80' deep and 5' wide.

MONO LAKE
Mile 62
Elevation 6,379' (and rising!)

The ancient lake, over 700,000 years old, is one of the oldest in North America; its approximate 60 square miles contain many unusual features. Throughout the centuries the combination of minerals and other salts being washed into the lake from the surrounding mountains and the evaporation of the freshwater from the lake have created a lake which is two and half times as salty and eighty times as alkaline as seawater. The soapy or slippery feel of the water today is the result of the alkaline which, incidentally, is very cleansing.

During the later part of the life of this lake, calcium bearing springs under the lake bed bubbling up through the briny sand on the lake bottom has created "tufa towers." These towers can only be created under the water. It is only when the water levels drops are the tufa towers visible.

During 1941 the city of Los Angeles began diverting water from the streams which led into Mono Lake. As a result of the source of water being kept from the lake the water level dropped some forty feet exposing many of the tufa towers The exposure to the wind, sand and sun began to change the shape and color of the exposed tufa.

The major effect of the drop on water level of the lake was the increase of the salt content of the water. In addition there were concerns over the ecological effect of the shrinking lake on the basin. Additionally, of the islands on the lake was no longer isolated from the shore due to the lower water level of the lake and predators had access to the birds which nested on the islands. Another effect of the receding water level were dust storms caused by exposure of more dirt.

MONO LAKE

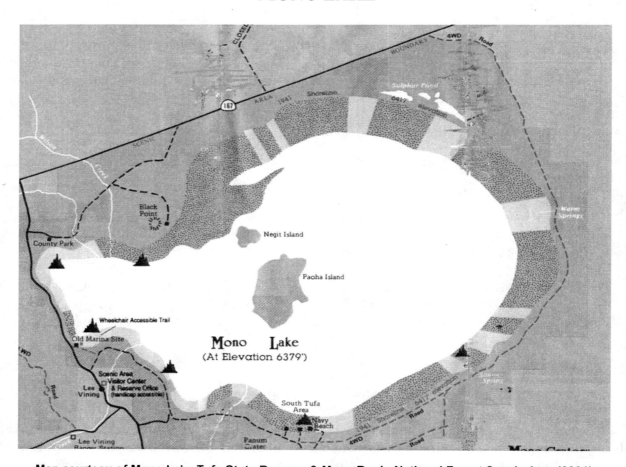

Map courtesy of Mono Lake Tufa State Reserve & Mono Basin National Forest Scenic Area (2001)

In 1994, after years of legal battles, a court order was issued to protect the lake and its tributary streams. As a result of the court decision the lake is to be increased in depth by 17 feet.

Part of the result of the increase in the depth of Mono Lake is that the deepening of the lake is once again covering some of the tufa towers. An extensive view of "uncovered" tufa towers can be found at Trona Pinnacles National Natural Landmark (Page 27 of this book.)

There is life in this seemingly "dead sea." Algae, brine shrimp and the alkali fly are the basis of a food chain which brings birds to the area. It is estimated that 50,000 California Gulls and 800,000-eared grebes along with some 80 other species of birds migrate to the Mono Basin annually. Approximately 90% if the California Gulls come from nesting at Mono Lake. No fish are able to survive in Mono Lake's water due to the heavy salt and alkaline content.

The alkali flies are quite unique. Most flies will pester humans and animal alike. The alkali fly will scurry ahead of you as you walk through the march. The Kuzedika Paiute sought the pupa stage of the alkali flies as they considered them a delicacy in their diet.

Activities in the Mono Basin include camping (There are no campgrounds in the preserve itself, they are located nearby) hiking, swimming in the lake, canoeing and kayaking.

Mono Lake area is administered by two government agencies. Mono Lake Tufa State Reserve administers portions of the land below 6,417 feet (The 1941 lake level.) The Mono Basin National Forest Scenic area administers an area in the Mono Basin of 116,00 acres.

The Scenic Area Visitor Center (and Reserve Office) is located on a hill which overlooks much of Mono Lake. Staffed with a personnel familiar with the Mono Basin and displays and information this is a "don't miss" for visitors interested in the Mono Lake and Basin area. The information center also offers canoe tours of the lake.

Information on numerous other guided tours of the area may be obtained here. These tours include sunset tours during the summer months and "tufa tours" year round. The visitor center is a "must see."

Mono Lake Tufa State Reserve, P.O. Box 99, Lee Vining, CA 93541, (760) 647-6331
monolk@Qnet.com
Mono Basin National Forest Scenic Area, P.O. Box 429 Lee Vining, CA 93541
Scenic Area Visitor Center (760) 647-3044
Lee Vining Ranger Station (760) 647-3000

ENTRANCE TO MONO LAKE COUNTY PARK (EAST)
Mile 66

This park is located alongside a small stream in an area which offers shade trees, toilets, picnic tables, drinking water and swings for the kids.

There is an easy trail and a boardwalk (new in 2001) wandering through the marsh and willows leading to the lake, pictured on page 67.

JUNCTION HIGHWAY 167 EAST/ LUNDY LAKE ROAD WEST
EAST ON HIGHWAY 167
ACCESS TO BLACK POINT (Mono Lake,) DIRT ROAD ACCESS TO BODIE STATE HISTORIC PARK, (21 Miles, Check for conditions.) HAWTHORNE, NEVADA (55 Miles)
Mile 68.5

Black Point is reached via a road located just east of Highway 395 leading south from Highway 167 east, or on a dirt road continuing east from the Mono County Park. It is advisable to check the condition of the road in the event there has been any recent inclement weather.

Black Point contains interpretive displays and is one of the more unusual areas found within the Mono Basin.

Some 13,000 years ago as the result of a volcanic eruption which occurred under the then 400-foot deeper lake, large fissures were formed. As a result of the lake's continuing to rise, some of these fissures are above ground today.

The fissures range from a few inches to a few feet in width and some are as much as 50 feet in depth. Some of the fissures may be explored today.

This state highway becomes Nevada State Highway 359 at the state line. This roadway reaches an altitude of 7592 feet. It is recommended that you check for conditions in winter.

WEST ON LUNDY LAKE ROAD

Lundy Lake Road follows Mill Creek 5 miles past several campgrounds to the foot of Lundy Lake, elevation 7,800 feet. (It is important to note that the campgrounds along the road are not associated with Lundy Lake Resort and the showers and other facilities found at the resort are for their guests and not for the public.)

Lundy/Lundy Lake: One of the most historic places in the valley is also one of the most scenic. Located just 5 miles west of Highway 395 at the head of Lundy Lake, in an area formerly occupied by the town of Lundy is the Lundy Lake Resort. Lundy Lake Resort (closed in winter) offers; lake and stream fishing, a general store, boat rentals, cabins, mobile homes, a trailer park with hook-ups and camp huts and camp sites. P.O. Box 550. Lee Vining, Ca 93541, (626) 309-0415. A deposit is required with reservations.

The picturesque Lundy Lake Resort

Lundy began life as a mining town in the late 1870's after gold discoveries in this deep canyon. Soon Lundy became a thriving and complete town. But the area was plagued by both avalanches and fires. By 1884 the high cost of mining the area forced the closure of the major mining projects in the area. Smaller mining attempts at mining continued here until the 1920's, none of which were successful.

Remains of the early town and its mining operations can still be found throughout the area, including the scattering of old mines in the hills above and behind Lundy Lake Resort.

The resort is right out of the past. There are no telephones and power is from a generator located on the property. Heat is by wooden stove in the cabins.

The lake and streams contain trout and the area contains numerous trails. Continuing 1 ½ miles through the camp and up the road are a series of Beaver Ponds and hiking trails. At the end of the road is parking for the trailhead and a vault toilet. **RV alert: This road is quite narrow and subject to pot holes which would be difficult to circumvent in a larger vehicle.**

One of the beaver ponds located along the road above Lundy Lakes Resort

RETURNING TO HIGHWAY 395, NORTHBOUND

Just north of the junction with Lundy Lake Road, Highway 395 begins a pretty steep climb. The road becomes 4 lanes as it climbs it way to its Conway Summit, the highest point on Highway 395 between Southern California and Canada.

The highway north of Conway Summit, to the Nevada border, is primarily 2 lanes with occasional passing lanes and several 4-lane sections.

THE MONO OVERLOOK NEAR CONWAY SUMMIT
(NOTE: ACCESSIBLE ONLY BY SOUTHBOUND TRAFFIC)
(Eastern Sierra scenic Byway)
Mile 73

A turnout/vista point on the southbound side of the highway, near Conway Summit, gives an excellent view of much of Mono Lake, Lee Vining on the far hill and the surrounding terrain.

CONWAY SUMMIT/ VIRGINIA LAKES ROAD (West)
Mile 74.
Elevation 8,138'
Gas, general store, (closed in winter)
ACCESS TO; VIRGINIA LAKES AREA, (8 LAKES IN TOTAL), DUNDERBERG ROAD, GREEN CREEK AND GREEN LAKE

Virginia Lakes area: Elevation 9,450' are 5 miles west of Conway summit at the end of Virginia Lakes Road, an all weather road. Virginia Lakes Resort, (760) 647-6484) closed in winter, is located on the north shore of Little Virginia lakes and in addition to lodging offers boat rentals (no gasoline motors are allowed on these lakes), a café, groceries, tackle and supplies. There is a campground located north of Little Virginia Lake near Trumbull Lake.

The Virginia Lakes area is in active use year round.

Fall at Big Virginia Lake finds snow on the bank and yes, a fisherman floating in the lake, bet he wears a wet suite!

Summer finds fishing, camping and hiking on the numerous trails accessible from the trailhead parking area. In winter the hills surrounding the lake are alive with cross-country skiers and snowmobiles while the anglers (during the season) are ice fishing through holes cut in the lakes

Dunderburg Road (#020) is located in the north side of Virginia Lakes Road, 4.5 miles west of Highway 395 and 1 mile east of Virginia Lakes. This dirt road offers access to Green Creek, Green Lake and in 11 miles joins Highway 395, 4.25 miles south of Bridgeport.

During non-inclement whether seasons this maintained road is passable by virtually any vehicle and addition to traveling through pine forests offers different views of the mountains surrounding the Bridgeport Valley and of Bridgeport itself.

LOOP TRIP
RETURNS TO HIGHWAY 395, 5 MILES SOUTH OF BRIDGEPORT

In addition to a "Scenic Route" into Bridgeport from Virginia Lakes, Dunderburg Road offers access to historic *Green Creek* and *Green Lake*.

Green Creek Road (#142) is 8 miles north of Virginia Lakes Road. One and one quarter miles north of Dunderburg Road is the location of a mill pond which was the site of a dynamo which was used to generate electrical power to the town of Bodie.

There is a "local" story regarding the transmission of the electricity from Green Creek to Bodie that we have heard from so many sources that I feel that is would inappropriate to not share it here. The lines from the generator on the millpond all of the way into Bodie were in a straight line. It was felt that if the power lines turned that the electricity would run off of the wire, so the story goes.

Along Dunderburg Road (#020)

This road follows Green Creek for 5.4 miles to a campground and trailhead parking area located below *Green Lake*.

There are numerous geographical sites in the area named "Dunderburg," the most significant at this time is Dunderburg Peak, altitude 12,374 feet. It appears that name was initially used in the area as the name for one of the more successful mines in the Dog Creek area. The name Dunderburg used in this area probably came from a Union man-of-war launched in 1865, which was named after a mountain in New York state, (Dunderburg is Dutch for "thunder mountain".)

RETURNING TO DUNDERBURG ROAD.

At a point 3 miles north of Green Lake Road, 11 miles north of Virginia Lakes Road Dunderburg Road ends at Highway 395.

At the junction of Dunderburg Road and Highway 395 there is a brass marker on a stone cairn the monument commemorates the location of the "Poor Farm."

In the mid-1880's Bodie Memorial Hospital was moved to this area and used as a refuge for the "aged, ill and penniless." After several years it was forced to close for financial reasons.

END OF VIRGINIA LAKES LOOP TRIP

* * * * * * * *

WE RESUME OUR TRIP ON HIGHWAY 395 AT CONWAY SUMMIT.

VIRGINIA CREEK *(Eastern Scenic Byway Site)*

Leaving Conway Summit the highway winds northward along the hills overlooking Virginia Creek located in a valley to the west.

During the fall the Aspens located in the valley present an array of vivid covers.

DOGTOWN
California Historic Landmark #792
(Eastern Sierra Scenic Byway)
Mile 79.5
(Pull-off, west side of Highway 395 just south of the junction of Highway 270, Bodie Road)
(Three monuments just south of highway junction)

Across the creek from the west side of the highway was the site of the first major gold rush on the eastern slope of the Sierra Nevada. The largest gold nugget found on the eastern side of the Sierra was found here.

The term "Dog Town" was a common miners term for a camp made up of huts or hovels.

Founded in 1857, there is not much to see here today. Piles of rock mark the site of this historic mining community.

These monuments mark the town of Dogtown located across Virginia Creek. A portion of the rubble from the town is seen to the left in this picture.

In this photo taken along the road to Bodie there are four deer can you spot them all?

HIGHWAY 270 EAST SIDE OF HIGHWAY 395
ACCESS TO BODIE STATE HISTORIC PARK

Mile 80
Altitude 8,369'
(7 Miles south of Bridgeport)
The park is located 13 miles east of Highway 395.
NO SERVICES, FLUSH TOILETS ONLY
(While the park is open all year weather conditions should be checked prior to traveling the road into Bodie during winter. **The road only is partially paved, in winter people do get stuck!**)
The park is open everyday from 8am to 7pm during the summer and 9am to 4pm in winter, or as posted. (Hours may vary due to weather and season)
FEE AREA
(760) 647-6445

A portion of downtown Bodie. The Methodist Church is in the foreground with the mill on the far hillside

Waterman S. Body discovered gold here in 1859. The initial gold rush on the western side of the Sierra Nevada Mountains was petering out and prospectors began searching the eastern side of the Sierras for the "elephant." "See the elephant" was slang at the time for searching for gold.

The spelling of the name was changed from Body to Bodie in an attempt to achieve correct pronunciation of the name.

The Standard Mill, which still stands on the hillside east of town, is closed to the public with the exception of tours, which are offered during the summer.

By 1879 the town of Bodie boasted of a population of some 10,000, which included women of ill repute, and numerous wicked souls. In 1881 Reverend F. M. Warrington described Bodie as "a sea of sin, lashed by the tempests of lust and passion."

One of the more infamous comments about Bodie came from an entry in a little girl's diary when she found she was moving to Bodie: "Goodbye God, I'm going to Bodie."

Not only were the killings and other wicked deeds a problem for Bodies' citizens, the weather at the 8,300+ foot altitude of the valley containing the town was extreme in the winter.

The initial mining boom was over in 4 years, so by 1882 the town was in decline. However some of the heartier souls hung on even though the larger mines were closing down as the cost of mining the gold and then transporting it out made Bodie less and less of a money making opportunity.

But, the town of Bodie took a long time to actually die. As late as the 1940's there were mining operations in the area.

The Standard Mill on the east side of Bodie. (Access by tour only)

In 1892 the first major fire ravaged the business district and in 1932 most of the northern portion of the town burned down.

As late as 1948, signs of life were reported from Bodie. The brick building (#58), next to the Odd Fellows Hall (#57), has been reported to have been used as an ice cream parlor/general store, possibly the last remaining business in this once bustling town

During the depression many of Bo die's citizens packed up what belongings they could carry and left the rest.

James Stewart Cain, resident of Bodie, had financed much of the real estate here.

The Cain residence (#6) the Methodist Church is in the background

As the citizens of Bodie who owed Cain money moved out, Cain would simply lock up the foreclosed property leaving all of the remnant personal belongings inside.

Subsequently, Cain hired a watchman to protect his secured property.

The Boone Store (# 36) with Kathy "window shopping" the historic merchandise. The outside wall is made of tin cans!

Today's visitor to Bodie is the beneficiary of Cain's protective efforts. The items that were left behind by the citizens of Bodie are now on display within the historic buildings making today's look at Bodies history even more complete. From the items to be found in the general store to the desks in the old school house to the furniture found in some of the houses, we are given a complete look at the historic Bodie, today.

In fact all of the items found in the town of Bodie today are authentic, with the exception of fire fighting equipment, trash receivers and the restrooms.

James Stuart Cain's personal residence (#6) is located on the northwest corner of Green & Park Streets and is easily recognized by the abundance of glass windows on the east side of the home. It is reported that Mr. Cain used the glass windows to grow plants, including fresh vegetables.

Thanks in great part to the efforts of the California State Park system, who in 1962 took over the management and maintenance of Bodie; the public today can walk the streets of yesterday. The Bodie that is seen today is in a state of "arrested decay."

While only about 10 % of the original Bodie stands today, it still remains the largest ghost town in the western United States.

There are two rangers and their families who live here full-time. There are other rangers who work here and commute from Bridgeport. This is one of the most isolated and desolate places within the state park system. The altitudes both at Bodie and on the road in are subject to heavy snow and winter weather conditions. The rangers use two snow-cats to get in and out for supplies during the winter season.

There are a total of four roads that find Body at their hub. All of these roads, with the exception of the partially paved highway, are un-paved and can be in pretty bad shape. Even with 4-wheel drive it is recommended that you check their condition before traveling them.

In 1929 a portion of a motion picture, "Hell's Heroes," was filmed in Bodie. The Bodie of that time can be seen in the movie.

This map printed from the California State Parks booklet "BODIE STATE HISTORIC PARK" shows the location of the buildings only in the central portion of Bodie. This booklet, which shows the location of all of Bodies buildings, may be obtained at various locations in the Mono Basin area or by writing: Bodie State Historic Park, P. O. Box 515, Bridgeport, CA 93517

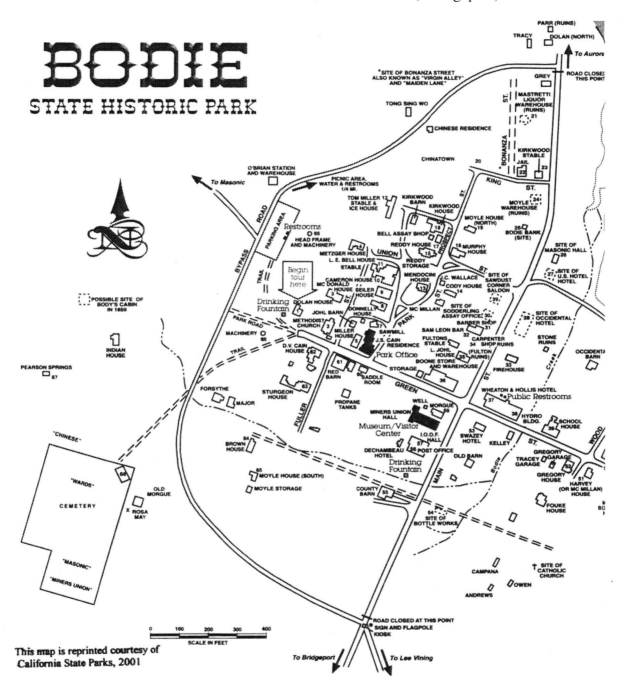

CLOSURE HOURS AT BODIE ARE STRICTLY ENFORCED FOR THE PROTECTION OF STRUCTURES AND ARTIFACTS. For information contact: Bodie State Park, P.O. Box 515, Bridgeport, CA, 93517, (760) 647-6445.

END OF SIDE TRIP

* * * * * * * *

WE RESUME OUR TRIP AT THE JUNCTION OF HIGHWAY 395 & HIGHWAY 270

JUNCTION DUNDERBURG/GREEN CREEK ROAD (West side of road)
Mile 82
This is the northern end of the Loop trip from Virginia Lakes Road described on Page 74

BRIDGEPORT RANGER STATION (east side of road)
Mile 87

Located one mile south of Bridgeport this ranger station is generally open weekdays. The annual "Adventures, the Recreation Guide" is available here and at various other locations throughout the Humboldt-Toiyabe National Forest area it is a very complete guide to adventuring in the area.

For information: Bridgeport Ranger Station, HCR 1 Box 1000, Bridgeport, CA 93517
(760) 932-7070, www.fs.fed.us/htnf/.

BRIDGEPORT (Altitude 6,468')
Mile 88
Full services

The Bridgeport Courthouse, in use since 1880

It is believed that the first white men in the area were fur trappers who traveled through the area in 1827. Originally called Big Meadows, this scenic town began life in the 1850's primarily as a supply town for the gold mining camps scattered throughout the area.

Today Bridgeport is the county seat for Mono County with its historic courthouse framed by a backdrop of one of the more rugged areas of the Sierra Nevada Crest. In 1880 the county seat for Mono County was moved here from Aurora, moved here when it was determined that Aurora was actually in the state of Nevada. The historic courthouse is open to visitors during normal business hours.

The Mono County Museum, located in the old school house, is open from Memorial Day through September 1 from 10 am to 5pm. Used as a schoolhouse from 1880 through 1964 the museum contains a complete history of the area and of Mono County.

Many of the businesses in Bridgeport are located in buildings which date back to the 1880's. Several of the Inn's have been in operation as such since that same time.

Bridgeport is surrounded by all forms of fishing from the East Walker River, which runs through town to the numerous lakes that surround the historic town.

The Bridgeport Museum is open daily during the summer

Much of Bridgeport can be seen in the 1947 motion picture "Out of the Past." which starred Kirk Douglas, Robert Mitchum and Jane Greer. Many of the downtown buildings in Bridgeport standing today are seen in the film.

Bridgeport Chamber of Commerce, P.O. Box 541, Bridgeport, CA 93517, (760) 932-7500, www.bridgeportcalifornia.com/.

The Bridgeport Reservoir, located just north of town offers good fishing from boat or shore. The Bridgeport Reservoir Recreation Area Marina and Campground offers RV and camping facilities, boat and/or slip rentals and guide services. *Bridgeport Reservoir Recreation Area,* P.O. Box 447, Bridgeport, CA 93517, (760) 932-7740, www.bridgeportmarina.net/.

TWIN LAKES ROAD
(East end of Bridgeport, South side of Highway 395
ACCESS TO TWIN LAKES RECREATION AREA (Elevation 7,092')
Fishing, boat launching rentals & docking, RV's, trailer and tent camping, cabins, gas, food, supplies
14 Miles

As Twin Lakes road leaves the town of Bridgeport on its way southwest towards the Twin Lakes area it reminds one of the World War II movies of ships making 90 degree turns to avoid a submarine attack.

Doc and Al's Robinson Creek Resort Is located in the woods seven miles from Bridgeport.

Located along Robinson Creek and near Buckeye Creek, both of which offers excellent fly-fishing, Doc and Al's additionally offers cabins, camping and RV spots.

Doc and Al's Robinson Creek Resort: P.O. Box 266, Bridgeport, CA 93517, (760) 932-7051.

The road leading into Doc and Al's ends at the Buckeye Campground and Buckeye Trailhead parking areas.

There are numerous camping areas from this point on as the road gently climbs through the aspen and pine trees into the deep valley containing the Twin Lakes.

Lower Twin Lakes Resort: Located 11 miles south west of Bridgeport on Twin Lakes Road this is a full service resort. Offering both lake and stream fishing this resort has been in operation since 1923. There are cabins available in addition to RV and trailer spots and camping.

The resort also offers a full service general store with everything from food, in the event you don't catch enough trout, to tackle and licenses enabling you to catch your dinner. There is also a deli in the store.

Boat rentals and moorage are also available, (there is a 5-mile per hour speed limit on Lower Twin Lake, they tell me that it makes the fish grow bigger here!) In 1985 the California record Brown Trout was caught here. It weighed 26+ pounds!

Additional fishing is found in other lakes and streams in the area located along well-marked trails.

Twin Lakes Resort: P.O. Box 248, Bridgeport, Ca 93517, (877) 932-7751
www.twinlakesresort.com,

At the junction of the twin lakes there is a large residential area known as "Twin Lakes Estates."

Upper Twin Lakes is the larger of the two lakes and is located further up the valley containing the two lakes. Upper Twin Lakes has no speed limit and, yes, you can water ski on this lake.

Mono Village is located at the head of Upper Twin Lake 14 miles southwest of Bridgeport at the end of Twin Lakes Road. This facility offers fishing, boat rentals launching and mooring, gas, lodging, a cafe, general store   No pets allowed.

Mono Village Marina located at the head of Upper Twin Lake

Mono Village began its resort life as "Maltby's Resort" in 1937. In 1952 Alpha and Norman Annett opened "Annett's Mono Village" and it continues to be operated by the Annett family.

One of the projects of the owners is to continue to stock the lake with their "home grown" browns and rainbow trout. When released at various time during the season, these trout are between three and eight pounds.

There are other lakes and streams within a short hiking distance from Mono Village. Deer hunting is also popular in the areas surrounding the "Village."

Annett's Mono Village Inc., P.O. Box 455, Bridgeport, CA 93517, (760) 932-7071 FAX (760) 932-7468, www.monovillage.com.

END OF SIDE TRIP TO TWIN LAKES

****

RETURNING TO HIGHWAY 395 AT BRIDGPORT

RESET MILEAGE TO "0"

Leaving Bridgeport, Highway 395 heads west before turning north again at the junction of Highway 108.

DEVIL'S GATE SUMMIT (Elevation 7,519')
Mile 11

**JUNCTION HIGHWAY 108, SONORA PASS
(CLOSED IN WINTER)**
Mile 17
Sonora 88 Miles, Full Services

Highway 108 crosses the Sonora Pass, elevation 9,924 feet in crossing the Sierra Nevada Mountains on its way to the town of Sonora, elevation 1,796, feet on the western slope of the Sierras.

SOUTHERN ENTRANCE TO WALKER CANYON
Mile 19
Fishing and camping

This is one of the more spectacular spots along Highway 395. This 10-mile section of the highway parallels the West Walker River through a spectacular canyon that the river has etched through the mountains in its process of dropping 1,400' in 14 miles.

Early morning snow clouds sit at the southern end of Walker River Canyon

While fires and floods will occasionally ravage this picturesque canyon, it always seems to retain its majesty and pure natural beauty.

EXIT WALKER CANYON AND ENTER ANTELOPE VALLEY
Elevation 5,300' +/=
Mile 29

At this point, the West Walker River leaves the confines of the canyon and flows through the widening Antelope Valley, one of five Antelope Valleys located in California.

The mild winter temperatures found in this valley were a major consideration involved in the founding of the 3 communities located here. The Sierra Nevada Mountains drives the Pacific rain clouds to 10,000 feet where they drop their rain, leaving the valley in a semi-arid rain shadow. In the late 1880's supply stops and centers for the mining towns found north and south of here started up in the towns located along the west side of the valley.

These rugged hills located behind the Meadowcliff Resort are a sharp contrast to the lush valley below

The lush pasturelands, ample water supply and the mild temperatures soon brought agriculture into the valley.

In addition to fishing the East Walker River, duck and deer hunting are also popular in the valley. The mountains surrounding the valley are popular with off roaders, mountain bikers, hikers and climbers.

Fall fills the valley with a variety of colors, thanks to the numerous Birch and Aspen trees. In the winter the valley becomes home for several herds of deer, in addition to being a winter nesting spot for bald eagles.

The communities of Walker, Coleville and Topaz each reflect their individual flavors to the traveler.

WALKER
Mile 30
Gas, food, general store, lodging, antiques, arts and crafts

The very first commercial building encountered on the south side of Walker is a TV center called H.F.U.. H.F.U.? "Hurray For Us!"

There are a variety of styles and modes found in the shops located in the Walker area. Many of the materials from the more talented artisans located in this center are shipped worldwide.

While there are "top end" retailers of arts, crafts and antiques found in Walker, there are curio and other shops to meet just about any visitor's budget.

The Outwest Native Gallery is the home of high quality Native American art.

Your author has personally caught some nice trout in the West Walker River within walking distance of Walker.

In 2002 the town of Walker was the scene of a tragedy shown on television, worldwide, when a fire fighting aircraft lost its wings when making a drop on a major fire, killing the crew, near the town.

The consensus in is that "All is well in the valley now," and "We are open for business as usual."

Located 4 miles north of the town of Walker is a resort called Meadowcliff. Meadowcliff offers a lodge, gift shop, restaurant and AN ESPRESSO BAR!

Originally opened in 1959, the new owners of Meadowcliff have expanded the resort and added the espresso bar, which is a favorite of locals and travelers alike. Located at the base of the picturesque cliffs, as pictured on page 87, the rooms offer sweeping views across the Antelope Valley, the West Walker River and the Sweetwater Mountains. The resort also offers a swimming pool and a playground for the kids, along with volleyball and a horseshoe area.

Meadowcliff Resort: 110437 Highway 395, Coleville, CA 96107, www.meadowcliff.com
(530) 495-2255

COLEVILLE
Mile 35
Antiques and crafts

Coleville is primarily a ranching community. Here there are additional opportunities for the antique and arts and craft seekers. Coleville, initially called "Centerville and occasionally "Doubletown" for the high prices that were found here, began life as a stage and freight stop

Coleville also has the closest Post Office to Walker.

TOPAZ
Mile 38
Arts and crafts

The town of Topaz is readily recognized as an arts and crafts center when driving through town on a spring or summer day. All forms of wind chimes, banners and flags wave at the highway traffic passing through Topaz.

Topaz is filled with mom and pop retail outlets offering a variety of locally produced arts and crafts.

INFORMATION WEB SITES FOR ANTELOPE VALLEY

Northern Mono Chambr of Comm. (530) 495-9666www.northernmonchamber@.com
Walker: www.walker.com , *Coleville:* www.colevillca.com , *Topaz Lake:* www.topazlake.com

JUNCTION HIGHWAY 89, MONITOR PASS
(CLOSED IN WINTER)
Mile 40
16 Miles to Hwy. 44, Markleeville 22 miles (services), 99 miles to Angels Camp & Hwy 49

This is the northern most of the three passes in our book connecting Highway 395 with the western side of the Sierra Nevada Mountains. All three of the passes are closed from the time of the first heavy snow until spring.

Highway 89 passes through the Monitor Pass, 8,314' altitude, as it heads westerly towards the more famous gold fields that opened California to the world in 1849.

The northern end of Antelope Valley, seen from Highway 89, east of Monitor Pass

LAKE TOPAZ
Mile 37
Fishing, boating, camping, picnic area and water skiing

Lake Topaz is located on the California/Nevada state line which allows anglers to fish with a license from either state.

Trophy rainbow and brown trout inhabit the lake with fishing allowed from January 1st to September 30th.

Most of the recreational facilities are located along the north side of the lake.

Late afternoon at Topaz Lake as seen from inside the Topaz Lodge and Casino

Our journey ends at the Lake Topaz Lodge and Casino. This resort offers the traveler the sort of amenities to be found in a Nevada Casino. Table games, slot machines, fast food and a dinner house are located in the Casino. Gas is available 24 hours a day. The lodge offers lake view rooms. *Topaz Lodge* (800) 962-0732, 1979 U.S. Highway 395 S., Gardnerville, NV 89410

LOOP TRIP "D" – FROM PAGE 66
HIGHWAY 120 EAST FROM LEE VINING TO BENTON HOT SPRINGS, BENTON, 46 MILES, BISHOP VIA HIGHWAY 6, 34 MILES, TOTAL TRIP 80 MILES
HIGHWAY 120 EAST, <u>CLOSED IN WINTER</u>

ATTRACTIONS:
Benton Hot Springs: Antiques, hot tub rentals (rent by hour or day) bed & breakfast, small general store and a historic townsite
Benton: Gas, food, lodging, general store.

This loop trip offers an alternative to the high traffic which quite often is found on Highway 395 in addition to giving the traveler a look at some of the other attractions in the area.

This loop trip takes the traveler through a portion of the Mono Lake National Forest Scenic Area, the northern portion of Inyo National Forest, through the Adobe Valley and two historic towns and down the Chalfant Valley at the foot of the White Mountains.

Just after passing the turnoffs to Panum Crater and to South Tufa Beach/Navy Beach, described on page 66, there is a gateway that is closed during winter when the roadway is impassible.

Highway 120 East starts a gentle climb towards Inyo National Forest passing through groves of pine trees.

At mile 12, the road passes through Big Sand Flat. The hillside from above the highway to the plain below resembles a giant ski run. The area is devoid of trees and all but small shrubs along several hundred feet of the highway.

Mile 16 is marked by Sagehen Summit, altitude 8,139'.

From mile 27 through mile 32 there are numerous roads leading off into what appears to be some popular 4 WD and off terrain vehicle areas.

This photo shows Nevada's tallest mountain, Boundary Peak, from mile 38 along Highway. 120

Black Lake, well named, can be seen on the east side of the road at mile 37.

Benton Crossing Road is at mile 38.5 on the west, or right side of the road. Benton Crossing Road gives access to the Owens River at Benton Crossing, 23 miles and to Highway 395 between Crawley and Convict Lakes, 29 miles.

As Yellow Jacket Road passes along the east side of Lake Crawley, it offers spectacular views of the Sierra Nevada Mountains and of Lake Crawley.

After passing the Benton Crossing Road junction, Highway 120 climbs a hill. There is a dirt road leading down the hill from the summit. From the junction of the dirt road much of the historic section of Benton Hot Springs can be seen on the hillside above the present community.

Not much is left of the older Benton as seen here today on the hillside above Benton Hot Springs

Benton Hot Springs history goes back to 1852 when the town was formed as a stagecoach stop and was called Benton. The hot springs located here were subsequently developed and other businesses began to flourish.

In 1862 Benton was the site of a major silver strike. The major strikes were in the Blind Spring Mining District, so named because the miners kept encountering unexpected springs as they dug. The mines in the area produced millions of dollars in silver of the next quarter of a century.

At one point Benton was the largest town in Mono County and rivaled the town of Bodie in many of her amenities.

The stagecoach stop, with displays is across from Benton Hot spring's "The Old House" antiques and hot tubs

When in the 1880's, the railroad located their station at a point 4 miles to the east of Benton; the old lady began to die. But she didn't die, not completely. Benton Hot Springs, as she became known when the town to the east not only took most of her population but also the name Benton, still has the hot springs and an awful lot of history and historical items, many of which are available for sale.

The Old House at Benton is one of the more interesting and unusual places that we have found to visit. The house itself is a reminder of the past. Not only is the house a reminder, virtually everything located in it dates back to yesteryear.

In addition to antiques The Old House is also the site of what are proclaimed as probably the purest hot springs anywhere. Hot tubs filled and cleaned after every use. The tubs are rented by the day or hour, by the person or for groups. Reservations are recommended.

There is also a bed and breakfast located in Benton Hot Springs. Information can be obtained through The Old House.

The Old House at Benton Hot Springs, 55045 Highway 120, Benton, CA 93512, (760) 933-2507

BENTON
food, supplies
Mile 46
Gas,

Four miles to the west Benton Hot Springs on Highway 120 is the town of Benton. This is also the end of Highway 120 east, where it ends at the Junction of U.S. Route 6, "The Grand Army of the Republic (Memorial) Highway." This meandering road used to go from coast to coast, Massachusetts to Long Beach California. This old highway now terminates in Bishop, the same place our journey terminates.

There are several restaurants located in Benton. The restaurant at the northwest corner of the junctions of Highways 6 and 120, Benton Station, also offers the traveler, a general store and a gasoline station. The restaurant and store are open from 7 am to 9 pm while the gas station is open 24-hours.

We found everyone in the Benton/Benton Hot Springs area to be friendly, and the gals at Benton Station, particularly Charlotte, gave us a wealth of information about the area.

There is also a market/general store south of the intersection of the two highways.

While initially our trip was planned to go directly south from Benton to Bishop, after talking with the ladies at Benton Station we decided to head north on Highway 6, into Nevada in search of wild horse herds which reportedly roamed the areas near Highway 6 in the area of Montgomery Pass. While we saw no horses we did get some spectacular views of the mountains surrounding Boundary Peak and of the peak itself.

Heading north on Highway 6 where is a casino and motel at the Nevada border, both of which appeared to be closed, on a Saturday afternoon!

Returning to Benton we headed south from there towards our destination of Bishop.

Just south of Benton on the west side of Highway 6 we spotted what appeared to be a small city or development of some sort. As we approached we realized that we were looking at a world-class junkyard. Covering some 40 acres Parkinson Auto Wrecking Yard must be one of the largest yards, anywhere, and it is located almost in the middle of nowhere!

As the road heads south through the Chalfont Valley the view widens out giving views of both the Sierra Nevada Mountains and of the White Mountains that loom above the highway.

Twenty miles south of Benton is the farming community of Chalfont. Chalfont has a general store.

At mile 30 the highway makes a sharp, 90-degree turn, to the west. Located just to the <u>east</u>, by making a left turn at the curve is Laws. Laws contains the Laws Train Museum as described on page 53 of this book. THERE IS NO SIGN FOR THE MUSEUM, OR LAWS ON THE SOUTHBOUND SIDE OF THE HIGHWAY.

Highway 6 ends at its intersection with Highway 395 at the north end of Bishop at mile 34.

This ends our journey and we sincerely hope that you have enjoyed these travels as much as we have in presenting them for you!

RV. PARKS
HESPERIA TO LAKE TOPAZ

HESPERIA
Desert Willow RV Resort
12624 Main St.*
HESPERIA CA 92345
(800) 900-8114
*Phelan Road, east off 395
(Phelan become Main St.)

RESERVATIONS AVAILABLE (Public)
OPEN ALL YEAR, 171 full hookup sites, pool, spa, rec. room, supplies, LP gas

Elevation 3,500'

SEE PAGE 3

ADELANTO
Adelanto RV Park
11301 Airbase Rd*
ADELANTO, CA 92301
(877) 246-5554
*Airbase Road WEST of 395

RESERVATIONS AVAILABLE (Good Sam)
OPEN ALL YEAR, 73 sites/40 full hookup, modems, CATV, dump, restrooms, showers, rec. room, mini mart w some supplies
Elevation 3,000'

SEE PAGE 3

RIDGECREST
Bertrand RV & Mobil Hone Park
Highway 178
2 miles east of 395
(760) 377-4000

RESERVATIONS AVAILABLE (Public)
OPEN ALL YEAR, 100 total/50 full hookups, CATV, dump

Elevation 2,700'.

SEE PAGE 8

RED ROCK CANYON STATE PARK
25 miles north of Mojave
SR 14 at Abbott Dr.
(661) 942-0662

NO RESERVATIONS (State Park)
OPEN ALL YEAR, dump station, max 30', primitive beautiful setting
Elevation 2,700'.

SEE PAGE 21

BALLARAT
4 miles east of Panamint
Valley road, 23 miles
North of Trona
NO PHONE, NO MAIL

NO RESERVATIONS (Public)
OPEN ALL YEAR, primitive with no services, no supplies, shower
Elevation 1,600'.

SEE PAGE 29

PANAMINT SPRINGS
SR 190, 50 miles
east of Lone Pine
30 miles west of
Stovepipe Wells
(760) 482-7680

RESERVATIONS RECOMMENDED (Public)
OPEN ALL YEAR, 12 sites full hook ups, gasoline, food service, mini-mart
Elevation 1,920'.

SEE PAGE 31

www.deathvalley.com

LONE PINE AREA:
Boulder Creek RV Resort
2550 South Highway 395
Lone Pine, 93545
(760) 876-4243
P.O. Box 870, Lone Pine, CA 93545

RESERVATIONS RECOMMENDED (GOOD SAM)
OPEN ALL YEAR, 55 full hook ups, restrooms, showers, modems, SATV, laundry, groceries, ltd supplies & LP gas, heated pool, spa, dump station, Rec. hall, playground
Elevation 3,700'.

SEE PAGE 13

www.395.com/bouldercreek

Lone Pine (Inyo National Forest)
7 miles west of Lone pine on
Whitney Portals Road
(760) 876 6200

NO RESERVATIONS (NFS)
OPEN APRIL – OCT. 43 paved sites RV / tent, pit toilets, 32' limit, firewood fishing, hiking
Elevation 6,000'

SEE PAGE 14

RV PARKS CONTINUED

LONE PINE AREA, CONT:
Whitney Portal
13 miles west of Lone
Pine on Whitney Portals Road
(760) 876-5542

    NO RESERVATIONS   (NFS)
OPEN MAY TO OCT. 43 paved sites RV/tent, chemical toilets, snack bar, 28' limit.
Elevation, 8,000'   SEE PAGE 15

INDEPENDENCE AREA
Onion Valley
13 miles west of
Independence on
Onion Valley Rd.
(760) 876-6200

    NO RESERVATIONS   (NFS)
OPEN JUNE – SEPT. 12 RV/tent & 17 tent, 28' limit, fishing, hiking
Elevation 9,200'.

    SEE PAGE 37

Tinnemaha Creek County Park
2..5 miles west of 395,
19.5 miles north of
Independence on Fish Springs Rd.
(760) 873-5577

    NO RESERVATIONS   (County)
OPEN ALL YEAR 15 RV, 37 tent sites, vaulted toilets, stream through campsite, fishing
Elevation, 4,000'.

BIG PINE AREA:
Grandview Campground
4 miles south of Ancient
Bristlecone Pine Forest
On access road from Hwy 168
(760) 873 -2500

    NO RESERVATIONS   (NFS)
OPEN MAY - NOV, 26 RV/tent spots, no water, trash or hook-ups, toilets, **no fee**, 34' limit
Elevation, 8,600'

    SEE PAGE 44

BISHOP AREA:
Keough's Hot Springs
Keough Hot Springs Rd.,
1 mile west of 395,
5 miles south of Bishop
(760) 872-4670

    RESERVATIONS RECOMMENDED   (Public)
OPEN ALL YEAR, 10 RV w/hook-ups, toilets, food service, pool & spa.
Elevation 4,350'.

    SEE PAGE 47

Parcher's Resort
South Lake Road,
6 miles south of Hwy. 168
(21 miles west of Bishop)
(760) 873-4177
www.bishopcreekresorts.com

    RESERVATIONS RECOMMENDED   (Public)
OPEN SUMMER ONLY, a few RV sites w/hook-ups, store, food service, fishing (lake & stream)
Elevation 9,260'.

    SEE PAGE 51

Sabrina
16 ½ miles west of
Bishop on SR168
(760) 873-2500
Reserveamerica (800) 444-7275

    RESERVATIONS RECOMMENDED   (NFS)
OPEN SUMMER ONLY, 9 RV sites, no hook-ups, 9 RV tent sites, 28' limit, no drinking water, groceries, fishing, boating
Elevation 9,000.

    SEE PAGE 52

Brown's Town Campground
Rt 1 Schober Ln., 50' west of 395
3 miles So. Of Hwy. 6
(760) 873-8522

    RESERVATIONS RECOMMENDED   (Public)
OPEN MARCH 1 THRU NOV. 30, 160 sites, 20 pullthroughs, hookups
Museum, store, laundry, showers, ltd RV supplies, food service, game room
Elevation 4200'

    SEE PAGE 48

RV PARKS CONTINUED

Brown's Millpond Campground　　RESERVATIONS RECOMMENDED　　(Public)
1.2 miles NW of Hwy 395　　OPEN MARCH 1 –OCT. 31, 60 dirt back ins, hookups, fishing, pond
4.5 miles N of Hwy 6　　restrooms, showers, security, playground, rec field, horseshoes
(760) 872-6911　　Elevation 4,500'　　SEE PAGE 48

ROCK CREEK AREA
French Camp　　SOME RESERVABLE SPOTS　　(NFS)
1 mile south of 395　　OPEN APR-NOV. 32 RV, no hook-ups, 86 total, 40' max, dump,
on Rock Creek Rd　　restrooms, on Rock Creek. NOTE: There are a total of 13 campgrounds
(exit 395 @ Tom's Place)　　with 300 sites along Rock Creek Road
(877) 444-6777　　Elevation 7,500'.　　SEE PAGE 57
www.rockcreeklake.com/camping/　　Reserveamerica (800) 444-7275

CROWLEY LAKE AREA
Crawley Lake　　NO RESERVATIONS　　(BLM)
5.5 miles south of Toms Place,　　OPEN APR-OCT 47 RV/trl, no hook-ups or slideouts. Toilets, dump
Crowley Lake Dr.　　fishing.,
on Lake Crowley　　Elevation 7,000'.
(760) 872-4881　　　　SEE PAGE 58

McGee Creek　　NO RESERVATIONS　　(NFS)
1 ½ miles west of　　OPEN JUNE-OCT. 28 RV/tent sites, 45' max., fishing
Hwy. 395 on McGee　　Elevation 7,600'.
Creek Rd,　　　　SEE PAGE 58
(760) 873-2500

BENTON CROSSING
Brown's Owens River Campground　　RESERVATIONS AVAILABLE　　(Public)
6 miles east of Hwy. 395 on　　OPEN APR.- OCT.50 RV/tent sites, restrooms, showers, mobile sewer
Benton Crossing Road　　service, groceries, food service, fishing, tackle.
(760) 920-0975　　Elevation 6,800'.　　SEE PAGE 58
219 Wye Rd, Bishop, CA 93514　　http://thesierraweb.com/recreation/browns/owens/html

CONVICT LAKE
Convict Lake　　NO RESERVATIONS　　(NFS)
2 miles west on Convict　　OPEN APR– OCT. 88RV/tent sites, 41' max. dump, restrooms,
Lake Road, from Hwy 395,　　lake fishing, boating (rental and mooring)
(760) 924-5500　　Elevation 7,600'.　　SEE PAGE 59

MAMMOTH LAKES – DEVILS POST PILE NATIONAL MONUMENT
Mammoth Mountain RV Park　　RESERVATIONS AVAILABLE　　(Public)
On SR 203, ½ mile east of　　OPEN ALL YEAR 165 RV sites, full hookups, dump station,
Old Mountain Road, 3 miles　　rest rooms with showers, indoor pool, spa, rec. room, RV supplies,
west of Hwy 395　　Across from the visitor center & ranger station.
(760) 934-3822　　Elevation 7,800'.　　SEE PAGE 61
P.O. Box 288, Mammoth Lakes, CA 93546　　www.gocampingamerica.com/mammothmountaim/index.html

JUNE LAKES LOOP
Pine Cliff Resort　　RESERVATIONS SUGGESTED　　(Public)
SR 158, 1 mile west of　　OPEN APR-NOV. 178 RV sites w/hookups, trlr. rentals, 60 tent sites
Highway 395 to　　showers, restrooms, groceries, tackle, laundry, fish, boat, food service.
Pine Cliff Rd., north 1 mile　　Elevation 7,800'.　　SEE PAGE 65
P.O. Box 38, June Lake, CA 93529　　www.rvpark.com/calif.htm　　(760) 648-7558

RV PARKS, CONTINUED

LEE VINING
Mono Vista RV Park
Located on Highway
395 in town

RESERVATIONS SUGGESTED (Public)
OPEN APR-OCT. 38 RV/tent w/hookups, restrooms, shower, dump, laundry, ltd RV supplies, tackle, playground, gift shop
Elevation 6,780'. SEE PAGE 68

P.O. Box 178, Lee Vining, CA 93541 (760) 647-6401

LUNDY LAKE
Lundy Lake Resort
5 miles west of Highway
395 at the head of Lundy
Lake
NO PHONES THERE

RESERVATIONS SUGGESTED (County)
OPEN MAY-OCT. 27 8 RV w/hookups (15 amp max) showers, restrooms, small store, fishing, boating hiking, no credit cards.
Elevation 8,000'. SEE PAGE 72
www.totalescape.com/destin/lakes/lundy

Reservations: P.O. Box 550, Lee Vining, CA 93541, Min $25,00 Deposit, Information (760) 309-0415

VIRGINIA/TRUMBULL LAKES AREA
Trumbull Lake Camp
5. miles west of Hwy 395,
north, right to campground,
(760) 932-7070

NO RESERVATIONS (NFS)
OPEN JUNE-OCT. 36 RV/tent sites (22' max), fishing, hiking
Elevation 9'500', SEE PAGE 74

BRIDGEPORT AREA
Willow Springs Motel & RV Park
Located 5 mile south of
Highway 395 on the east
side of the highway.
P.O. Box 1040, Bridgeport, CA 93517

RESERVATIONS SUGGESTED (Public)
OPEN APR-OCT. 27 full hookups (no slide outs). Restrooms, showers, laundry, pond, near Bodie Ghost town.
Elevation 6,800'. SEE PAGE 82
(760) 932-7725

Paradise Shores RV Park
On SR 182, 2.8 miles
North of Highway 395
At the Bridgeport Reservoir
P.O. Box 477, Bridgeport, CA 93517

RESERVATIONS SUGGESTED (Public)
OPEN MAY-OCT. 39 RV sites, full hookups, central modem, CATV, restrooms w showers, dump, fishing, tackle, boating, (ramp & rentals)
Elevation 6,500'. SEE PAGE 83
www.bridgeportmarina.com (760) 932-7735

TWIN LAKES AREA
Twin Lakes Resort
10 miles southwest of
Bridgeport on Twin Lakes Rd.
(on Lower Twin Lake)

RESERVATIONS SUGGESTED (Public)
OPEN APR-OCT 16 RV sites, full hookups, restrooms, showers, laundry, (boat & dock rentals) fishing, general store, deli, cabins.
Elevation 7,100'. SEE PAGE 84

P.O. Box 248, Bridgeport, CA 93517 www.twinlakesresort.com (800) 407-6153
Mono Village
14 miles southwest of
Bridgeport on Twin Lakes Rd.
(on Upper Twin Lake)

NO RESERVATIONS (Public)
OPEN APR-OCT. 39 RV sites, full hookups, modem, CATV, gas, rest rooms, showers, dump, laundry, gen. Store, gas, food service, fishing, boat & dock rentals, boat ramp,
Elevation 7,100'. SEE PAGE 84

P.O. Box 466, Bridgeport, CA 93517 www.monovillage.com (760) 932-7071

Topaz Lake RV Park
¾ mile south of the Nevada
state line on the south shore
of Topaz Lake
(530) 495 2357

RESERVATIONS SUGGESTED (Public)
OPEN MARCH-OCT. 54 RV sites, full hookup, modems, CATV, restrooms, showers, laundry, ltd groceries & supplies, lake swimming, fishing, tackle, boat ramp & dock
Elevation 5,000'. www.topazlakepark.@aol.com SEE PAGE 90

SOME CAMPING GUIDELINES

Whether in the desert or in the mountains we have found that by camping on our journeys we have found that we gain just a little bit extra during our travels

There are somewhere in the neighborhood of 650 campgrounds located in California, with a great number of them located within the areas covered in this book.

While some campgrounds are listed herein, it is not our intent to create a camping guide. We have listed below the reservation sources for the federal and state campgrounds. It is our suggestion that you contact the auto clubs or RV clubs for a more complete list.

Because of fluctuation our policy to not include specific prices for anything in our books.

GOVERNMENTAL CAMPGROUND RESERVATION SOURCES

CALIFORNIA STATE PARKS
(Reservation and cancellation fees)
Reserve America: (800) 444-7275, www.ReserveAmerica.com

NATIONAL PARKS & MONUMENTS
(Cancellation fees)
Biospherics; (800) 365-2267

YOSEMITE RERVATIONS
(All Yosemite Campgrounds require Reservations, made up to 5 months in advance)
(800) 436-7275
http://reservations.nps.gov

NATIONAL FOREST AND ARMY CORPS OF ENGINEERS
(Reservation and cancellation fees)
NRRS (877) 444-6777, http://Reserveusa.com

ITEMS YOU MAY WISH TO TAKE ALONG

We have compiled the items listed below as the result of numerous camping and day trips into not only the desert but also in the mountains.
Flashlight, waterproof matches, toilet paper, hatchet, pocketknife, and food for 3 days.

Warm clothes (it can really get cold here at night), hat, sunglasses, sunscreen, first aid kit, lip balm, good walking shoes and a snakebite kit.

Surplus style trenching shovel and 4 boards 1" X 12" X 16" for driving out of sand.

A radio (channel 9 is monitored in most of these areas) or cellular telephone (911 is the emergency number for most of the area) Warning! There are areas of "no reception" cell phones in many places.

Have your vehicle checked before leaving home and be aware of the mileage range of your vehicle because gas stations can be few and far between.

In addition to these items, it doesn't hurt to take that camping gear even if your intentions are not to camp out. In particular we always carry a 6' X 8' canvas shade awning and the poles on our day trips in addition to our camping trips.

Don't forget to include binoculars, bird/plant/animal guide books and of course your camera. When taking pictures it is best to remember that while in the desert your best pictures will generally be taken early or late in the day. It is not a bad idea to look at different lens filters than you might be using elsewhere.

If you will be out at night a star chart might be an idea. The air is so clear you will probably see stars that you have never seen before. Some campgrounds, including Red Rock Canyon, actually post monthly star charts to aid in your viewing.

CAMPING

In most forest areas camping is only allowed in designated campground. In some of the desert areas, in particular those lands under the jurisdiction of the Bureau of Land Management (BLM), camping is permitted outside of regular campgrounds with the restriction listed below.

In none of the areas covered in this book is gathering or cutting of firewood permitted, YOU MUST BRING YOUR OWN FIREWOOD.

Shooting firearms in ANY inhabited or public use areas is prohibited.

In areas outside of the campgrounds, you are required to obtain a campfire permit from April through October. These permits are free and can be obtained at California BLM offices, or from BLM Rangers.

Never camp within 1000 feet of water sources. Wildlife and cattle need the water access.

Keep your vehicle within 25 feet of existing roads, in existing campsites.

Do not camp in washes, these areas are prone to flash floods at <u>anytime.</u>

If you brought it in, YOU PACK IT OUT.

Do not dig pit toilets, (a 3" to 4" shallow spot is OK). Do not drain holding tanks.

Never camp within, or immediately adjacent to ruins or other structures.

CAMPING GEAR

The selection of camping gear can be quite personal. What we have listed here are the items which we have found, through experience, best serve our wants and needs.

We looked at our camping gear with a twofold purpose. We live in an area in which a great deal of earthquake activity has recently occurred. Consequently we have looked at our camping equipment as a portion of our "earthquake survival package"

Tent: For the two of us we use a 8' X 8' dome tent, it has plenty of room and offers the least wind resistance. Your tent should have a "tub" bottom and have the ability to completely close. This is to keep the "critters" out. NOTE: Experience has taught us to use rocks or other heavy objects on top of the tent stakes. Generally speaking sand does not have the best holding characteristics and the desert is prone to some pretty high winds.

Ground Cloth: Goes under the tent for protection of the material and acts to insulate.

Air Mattress: A five-inch thick queen-size air mattress with an electric or a foot pump is a real comfort.

Bedding: An opened sleeping bag atop the air mattress with queen-size waterbed sheets (joined) with one or two sleeping bags on top makes for comfortable sleeping.
The sleeping bag on top of the air mattress is used for insulation.

Canvas Awning: We use 6' X 8' canvas awning that is rigged on expandable aluminum poles from the top of our vehicle. This offers protection from sun and rain.

Lantern: In addition to a Coleman style lantern we also bring 2 flashlights into the tent, one each in the event we need to both make that "trip" at the same time!

Cooking Equipment: We use a two-burner SELF-LIGHTING propane cylinder stove and a small portable barbecue. The self-lighting stove ALWAYS GOES ON!

Kitchen Box: A large lidded box that contains frying pans, saucepans, and a cutting board kitchen knife, silverware, paper plates & bowls, paper towels, can opener, trash bags, spatula & other cooking utensils. It also contains citronella candles that help keep the bugs away.

Ice Chest: We bring several smaller chests and one large one. This keeps us out of our main ice chest when we are looking for incidentals.

INFORMATION POINTS INCLUDING: MUSEUMS, VISITORS CENTERS WEB SITES AND OTHER SOURCES

(Operating times shown believed correct and are subject to change. Most facilities shown are closed on Christmas, and possibly other holidays, call entity for further information.)

Ancient Bristlecone Pine Schulman Grove Visitor Center   (Usually open Mid-May to
23 miles east of Bishop via Hwy 168 & White Mountain Rd.   December)
(760) 873-2500 (U.S.F.S. –Bishop)
www.r5fs.fed.us/inyo/wc/bcp/

Big Pine Chamber of Commerce and Visitors Center   Tues – Thurs 9:30 - 5
126 South Main St.   Friday, Saturday 9 - 6
P.O. Box 23
Big Pine, CA. 93513
(760) 938-2114
www.bigpine.com

Bishop Chamber of Commerce & Visitors Bureau   Daily 9 -5
690 N. Main St.
Bishop, CA 93514
(760) 873-8405
www.bishopweb.com

Bodie State Historical Park   Mem. Day to Labor Day = 9 - 7 Winter 9 - 4
P.O. Box 515   (The Park is13 Miles east of Hwy 395 between Mono Lake & Bridgeport)
Bridgeport, CA 93517
(760) 647-6455   (Note, closure hours STRICTLY enforced!)
http://ceres.ca.gov/sierradsp/bodie.html

Death Valley Chamber of Commerce   Daily
118 Highway 127
Shoshone, CA. 92384
(760) 852-4524
http://www,deathvalleychamber.org/

Death Valley National Park   Daily
P.O. Box 570
Death Valley, CA. 92328
(760) 786-3200
http://www.nps.gov/deva/pphtm/facilities.html

Eastern California Museum   Daily 10 - 4
155 North Grant St. (West of Courthouse)   Except Tues.
Independence, CA 93526
(760) 878-0258
www.lonepinechamber.org/siteseeing/museum.html

Eastern Sierra InterAgency Visitor Center — Daily
Highway 395 at Highway 136 (2 miles south of Lone Pine)
P. O. Box R
Lone Pine CA 93545-2017
(760) 876-6222
www.r5.fs.fed.us/inyo/mtwhitney

Jawbone Station Visitor Information Center (BLM) — Daily
Jawbone Canyon Road
(17.5 miles north of Mojave, 1 ½ mile south of Red Rock/Randsburg Road)
(760) 373-1146
http://www.jawbone.info/station.html
Email: jawbone@ccis.com

Laws Railroad Museum — Daily 10 - 4
6 miles north of Bishop on Hwy 6 @ Silver Canyon Rd.
P.O. Box 363
Bishop, Ca 93515
(760) 873-5950
www.thesierraweb.com/bishop/laws/

Mammoth Ranger Station & Visitors Center — All-year Daily 8 – 5
Highway 203, 3 miles west of Highway 395
P.O. Box148
Mammoth Lakes, CA 93546
(760) 924-5500
www.r5.fs.fed.us/inyo/siteindex.htm

Mammoth Lakes visitors Bureau & Central Reservations — Mon – Fri 8 - 5
P.O. Box 48
Mammoth Lakes, CA 93546
(888) 466-2666 (Weather & Road conditions (800) 427-7623)
www.VisitMammoth.com

Maturango Museum & Northern Mojave Visitor Center — Daily 10 - 5
100 E, Las Flores Ave.
Ridgecrest, CA 93555
(760) 375-6900
www.maturango.org
Email Matmus1@ridgenet.net

Mojave River Valley Museum — Daily 11- 4
270 E. Virginia
Barstow, CA 92311
(760) 256-5452
http://mvm.4t.com

Mono Basin Scenic Area Visitor Center Open all year
West Shore of Mono Lake Weekends in Winter
P.O. Box 429
Lee Vining, CA. 93541
(760) 647-3044
www.r5.fs.fed.us/inyo/siteindex.htm

Mono Lake Committee Information Center Daily 9 – 7:30
Highway 395 & 3rd St.
P.O. Box 29
Lee Vining, CA. 93541
(760) 647-6595
www.monolake.org/monomap/mk.htm

Mount Whitney Ranger Station Open year-round
Highway 395, south end of Lone Pine Staffed only spring - fall
P.O. Box 8
Lone Pine, CA 93545
(760) 876-6200
www.r5.fs.fed.us/inyo/siteindex.htm

Piute Shoshone Indian Cultural Center 10 – 4 "most days"
2300 West Line St.
Bishop, CA 93514
(760) 873-9478

Red Rock Canyon State Park Visitor Center Daily
Highway 14 at Abbot Drive
Cantil, CA. (no mail)
Red Rock Canyon Interpretive Association
P.O. Box 848
Ridgecrest, CA. 93556
http://www.calparksmojave.com/redrocks/
http://areas.wilderness.com/ (California State Parks reservations & info.)

Route 66 Museum Fri. – Sun. 10 - 4
681 First Ave. (Harvey House)
Barstow, CA 92317
(760) 255-4890
www.barstow66museum.itgo.com

Searles Valley Historical Society (Mon.,Wed.,Thurs, Sat. 9 am-Noon Tues.,Fri. 10 am-1pm)
P.O. Box 630 (Other times by appointment)
Trona, CA 93592
(760) 372-5222
www.1.iwvisp.com/svhs/brochure.html

Old Guest House Museum, Trona (Searles Valley) Sat. & other days,
13193 Main Street Hours vary, call first
Trona, CA 935-5222
(760) 772-4800, 3724230
www.trona-ca.com/points.htm

U. S. Bureau of Land Management (BLM) Mon – Fri 8 - 5
300 Richmond Road
Ridgecrest, CA 93555
www.ca.blm.gov/index.html
Email: lsolway@ca.blm.gov

U.S.D.A. Forest Service Mon – Fri 8 - 5
798 W. Main St.
Bishop, CA 93514
(760) 873-2500 (Recorded messages)
www.fs.fed.us/

The U.S. Naval Museum of Armament and Technology Weekdays 10 - 4
1 Pearl Harbor St. (end of Blandy St.)
Ridgecrest, CA 93555
(760) 939-3530
www.chinalakemuseum.org/

Victor Valley Museum Weds – Sat 10 - 4
11873 Apple Valley Rd. Sun 12 - 4
Apple Valley, CA 92308
(760) 240-2111
www.vvmuseum.com

White Mountain Ranger Station Open all year,
798 Main St. Mon – Fri. in Winter
Bishop, CA 93514
(760) 873-2500
www.r5.fs.fed.us/inyo/siteindex.htm

INFORMATIVE WEB SITES

www.395.com The High Sierra web page

http://thesierrawebpage.com The Eastern Sierra Web Page

www.donaldlaird.com/landmarks/ California State Historic Land Marks (Private site)

INDEX

ELANTO	3
AGUEREBERRY CAMP/POINT	30
ALABAMA HILLS	14
ALTITUDE	b
ANCIENT BRISTLECONE FOREST MAP	43
ANCIENT BRISTLECONE FOREST	42
ANTELOPE VALLEY (MONO CNTY)	87
ASPENDELL	52
BAKERSFIELD	25
BALLARAT	26, 29
BARSTOW	4
BEARS	c
BEATTY, NEVADA	46
BENTON	58, 93
BENTON CROSSING	64, 91
BENTON CROSSING ROAD	58, 91
BENTON HOT SPRINGS	58, 92, 90
BIG PINE	41, f
BIG PINE CHAMBER	41
BIG SAND FLAT	91
BISHOP	9, 39, 48, 90, 94
BISHOP MULE DAYS	48
BISHOP AREA CHAMBER	49
BISHOP CITY PARK	f
BISHOP CREEK CANYON	49
BISHOP CREEK RECREATIONAL AREA	50
BISHOP CREEK LODGE	50
BLACK LAKE	91
BLACK POINT	72
BLIND SPRING MINING DISTRICT	92
BLM BISHOP OFFICE	49
BLM OFFICE, RIDGECREST	27
BODIE STATE HISTORIC PARK	72, 78 – 81
BODIE STATE HISTORIC PARK (MAP)	81
BORON	4
BOUNDARY PEAK	91, 93
BRIDGEPORT	82
BRIDGEPORT COURTHOUSE	82
BRIDGEPORT PARK	f
BRIDGEPORT RANGER STATION	82
BROWN'S OWENS RIVER CAMPGRND	58
BURRO SCHMIDTS TUNNEL	22, 24
BURRO SCHMIDT TUNNEL (MAP)	23
CAJON SUMMIT	3
CAMPING GUIDELINES	99
CARDINAL RESORT	52
CERRO GORDO	11
CERRO GORDO MINE	33, 35
CHALFONT	94
CHINA LAKE NVL AIR WEPS CENTER	8, 11
CHINA LAKE ROAD	7
COLEVILLE	88
COTTONWOOD CHARCOAL KILNS	12
CONVICT LAKE	59
CONWAY SUMMIT	74
COSO JUNCTION	11, e
CRAWLEY LAKE	56, f
CRAWLEY LAKE ACCESS	58
CRAWLEY LAKE DRIVE	56, 58
CRAWLEY LAKE VISTA POINT	58
CHINA LAKE	25
CRESTVIEW CALTRANS REST AREA	64, f
"CURES"	e
DARWIN	32
DARWIN FALLS	32
DEADMAN'S SUMMIT	65
DEATH VALLEY	4, 11, 29, 30, 31, 36, 44, 46
DESERT MUSEUM	5
DEVIL'S GATE SUMMIT	86
DEVILS POSTPIL NTL MONUMENT	56, 61, 63
DIAZ LAKE	e
DIRTY SOCKS HOT SPRINGS	11, 32, 36
DIVISION CREEK CALTRANS REST STP	40, f
DOC & AL'S ROBINSON CRK RESORT	83
DOGTOWN	76, f
DOBY CORNERS	3
DUNDERBURG ROAD	56, 75
DUNDERBURG MTN.	76
DUNDERBURG MINE	76
EAST WALKER RIVER	86 – 88, g
EASTERN CALIFORNIA (SIERRA) MUSEUM	17, 18, e
EASTERN SIERRA SCENIC BYWAY	e
EL MIRAGE DRY LAKE	3, 4
EL PASO MOUNTAINS	7
EUREKA DUNES	44
EUREKA MINE	30
FATHER CROWLEY POINT	32
FORT INDEPENDENCE	9, 40, 41
FOSSIL FALLS	10
FREMONT VALLEY	7
GLACIER LODGE/GLACIER LDG HWY	41
GLACIER LODGE RESORT	41
GLASS FLOW ROAD	65
GOLDFIELD, NEVADA	42, 46
GRANT LAKE	65
GRAY'S MEADOW	37
GREEN CREEK/LAKE	75
GULL LAKE	65
HAWTHORNE, NEVADA	72
HESPERIA	3
HIGHWAY 6 (U.S)	53, 93
HIGHWAY 14	8, 10, 14, 20, 25

HIGHWAY 89 WEST (MONITOR PASS)	89
HIGHWAY #95 (NEVADA)	46
HIGHWAY 108, SONORA PASS	86
HIGHWAY 120 WEST (TIOGA PASS)	68
HIGHWAY 120 EAST	66, 91
HIGHWAY 136	13
HIGHWAY 158 WEST (NORTH JUNCTION OF JUNE LAKES LOOP)	68
HIGHWAY 167 EAST	72
HIGHWAY 168	42, 43, 49 - 52
HIGHWAY 178 WEST	25, 27
HIGHWAY 178, EAST	26
HIGHWAY 190	11, 30, 32, 36
HIGHWAY 203 (SOUTH END OF MAMMOTH LAKES SCENIC DRIVE)	61
HIGHWAY 395, HISTORY	d
HILTON CREEK	57
HOT CREEK FISH HATCHERY	60
HOT CREEK GEOTHERMAL SITE	60
HOT CREEK FLY FISHING RANCH	60
HOT SPRINGS ROAD	64
HUMBOLT-TOIYOBE NTL FOREST	82
INDEPENDENCE	9, 18
INDEPENDENCE DEHY PARK	e
INDEPENDENCE TO BISHOP (MAP)	39
INDIAN VALLEY ROAD	7, 22
INTERAGENCY VISITORS CENTER	13, e
INYOKERN ROAD	8
INYO MOUNTAINS	15, 32
INYO NATIONAL FOREST	91
INYO NTL FOREST, FOREST SERVICE	45
JAWBONE CANYON/ BLM INFO CNTR	20
JOHANNESBURG	5
JUNE LAKES	65
JUNE LAKE LOOP (SOUTH END	65, f
JUNE LAKE CHAMBER	65
JUNE LAKE VILLAGE	65
KEARSARGE CANYON	18
KEARSARGE PASS TRAIL	38
KEELER	11, 33, 35, 42, 53
KEOUGH'S HOT SPRINGS	47
KENNEDY MEADOWS	10
KERN RIVER	25
KRAMER/KRAMER JUNCTION	3, 6
LAKE ISABELLA	7, 10, 25
LAKE SABRINA	52
LAKE SABRINA RECREATION AREA	49
LAKE TOPAZ	90, g
LAS VEGAS	46
LAWS	53, 94
LAWS RAILROAD MUSEUM	42, 53, 94
LEE VINING	58, 68
LITTLE LAKE	10
LITTLE LAKES VALLEY ACCESS	56
LOGGING CAMP ROAD	65
LONE PINE	11, 32
LONE PINE, CITY OF	13
LONE PINE CHAMBER	14
LONE PINE CREEK	15
LONG VALLEY	64
LOOP SIDE TRIP "A"	20
LOOP SIDE TRIP "B"	26
LOOP SIDE TRIP "C"	36
LOOP TRIP "D"	90
LOS ANGELES AQUEDUCT	9
LUNDY LAKE ROAD	72
LUNDY/LUNDY LAKE	72
LUNDY LAKE RESORT	72
MAMMOTH LAKES	56, 61, 63, f
MAMMOTH SCENIC DR NORTH END	64
MANZANAR NTL HISTORIC SITE	17, e
MANZANAR NTL HISTORIC SITE (MAP)	16
MARKLEEVILLE	89
MATURANGO MUSEUM	8
MAZOURKA CANYON	18
MCGEE CREEK/ROAD	58
MEADOWCLIFF	88
METHUSELAH TREE	45]
MONITOR PASS (HIGHWAY 89 WEST)	89
MONO CRATERS	66, f
MONO BASIN HISTORICAL MUS.	69
MONO BASIN VISITOR CNTR	71
MONO COUNTY (NORTH) CHMBRS	89
MONO COUNTY MUSEUM	83
MONO LAKE	66, 67 – 72, a
MONO LAKE COUNTY PARK	72
MONO LAKE NATIONAL FOREST	91
MONO OVERLOOK	74, e
MONO VILLAGE	84
MONTGOMERY PASS	93
MOJAVE	4, 20
MOUND HOUSE, NEVADA	42
MOUNT WHITNEY FISH HATCHERY	40
NATIONAL TRAILS HIGHWAY (ROUTE 66)	4
NAVY BEACH	67, 91
OLANCHA	11, 32
OLD HOUSE, THE BENTON HOT SPRINGS	92
OLD OWL INN (THE)	6
ONION VALLEY	19, 37
OPAL MINING	22
OWENS LAKE	9, 11, 12, 32, 35, 42, 53
OWENS RIVER	9, 91
OWENS RIVER ROAD	60
OWENS RIVER ROAD, NORTH END JNCTN	64
OWENS RIVER RANCH	64
OWENS RIVER RANCH	64
OWENS VALLEY	4, 8, 9
OWENS VALLEY OVERLOOK	f
OWENS VALLEY PIUTE/SHOSHONE CULTURE CENTER	49
OWENS VLY RADIO OBSERVATORY	46
PANAMINT	26

PANAMINT MOUNTAINS	30	SILVER LAKE	65
PANAMINT VALLEY	28, 29	SLIM PRINCESS	42
PANAMINT VALLEY ROAD	30	SOUTH LAKE	51
PANAMINT SPRINGS RESORT	11, 31	SOUTH MONO LAKE AREA	66
PANUM CRATER	91	SOUTH TUFA	66
PANUM AND MONO CRATERS	66	SPANGLER HILLS	26
PARCHER'S RESORT	51	STATE RANGE PASS	28
PATRIARCH GROVE	45	STOVEPIPE WELLS CENTER	11, 30
PEARBLOSSOM/PALMDALE HWY	3	SOUTH TUFA BEACH	91
PEARSONVILLE	10	SWANSEA	11, 35
RAINBOW CANYON	32	TIOGA PASS ROAD (HWY 120 WEST)	68
RAINBOW PACK STATION	51	TOM'S PLACE	56, 57
RAND, THE	5	TONOPAH, NEVADA	58
RAND MOUNTAINS	3	TOPAZ	89
RANDSBURG	4, 5, 20, 26	TRONA	28
RANDSBURG RAILROAD	6	TRONA MUSEUM	28
RANDSBURG ROAD	20	TRONA ROAD	7, 26
RANDSBURG/REDROCK CANYON ROAD	7, 2	TRONA PINNACLES NATL LANDMARK	27
RED MOUNTAIN	5, 6, 26	TRONA-WILDROSE ROAD	27, 28, 30
RED ROCK CANYON STATE PARK	21	TUOLUMNE MEADOWS	68
RED ROCK INYOKERN ROAD	22	TURNBULL LAKE	74
RIDGECREST	7, 8, 25	TWIN LAKES RECREATIONAL AREA	83 - 85
ROAD INFORMATION	b	TWIN LAKES ROAD	83
ROBBER'S ROOST	24	TWIN LAKES RESORT	84
ROCK CREEK ROAD	57	VICTORVILLE	3
ROCK CREEK LAKE	57	VIRGINIA CREEK	76, f
ROCK CREEK RESORT	57	VIRGINIA LAKES	74
ROCK CREEK LODGE	57	VIRGINIA LAKES ROAD	56, 74
ROUND VALLEY	f	WALKER	88
RV CAMPSITES	95	WALKER CANYON	86
RYOLITE, NEVAVDA	46	WEATHER INFORMATION (LOCAL)	b
SAGEHEN SUMMIT	91	WEST LINE STREET (BISHOP)	49
SALINE VALLEY	44	WHITE MOUNTAIN ROAD	44
SCHULMAN GROVE	42, 45	WHITE MOUNTAINS	58, 94
SEARLES DRY LAKEBED	28	WHITMORE HOT SPRINGS	58
SEARLES STATION CUT-OFF	26	WHITNEY PORTAL	15
SEARLES VALLEY	26	WHITNEY RANGER STATION	15
SEVEN PINES	37	WILDROSE CANYON ROAD	30
SHADOW MOUNTAIN ROAD	4	WILDROSE CHARCOAL KILNS	30
SHERWIN CREEK ROAD	60	YELLOW ASTER/RAND MINE	5
SHERWIN GRADE PULL-OUT	56, f	YOSEMITE NATIONAL PARK	68
SHERWIN SUMMIT	56	ZURICH STATION	42
SIERRA VIEW VISTA POINT	44		